Martha McCulloch Williams

The Capital Cook Book

Martha McCulloch Williams

The Capital Cook Book

ISBN/EAN: 9783744795197

Printed in Europe, USA, Canada, Australia, Japan

Cover: Foto ©Lupo / pixelio.de

More available books at **www.hansebooks.com**

THE

✣Capital✣Cook✣Book✣

COMPILED FROM ORIGINAL AND TESTED RECIPES.

MRS. MARTHA M. WILLIAMS.

FRANK L. LINK,
MONROE CITY, MO.
1895.

Introduction.

In presenting this book, it is given with a view to assisting the inexperienced, and also those who have already acquired the knowledge of cooking. There is always a desire on the part of housekeepers to excel in this part of their work, and there may be some suggestions that will aid them. By following the directions explicitly, the inexperienced sister will be enabled to have the culinary department of her home equal to those of the ladies who have had better advantages in this part of their training. System is indispensable in everything in which we engage, and surely there is nothing more essential to the mothers and wives of our land, than to be excellent cooks, as no one objects to a well prepared meal. Believing that with these words of introduction The Capital Cook Book will commend itself to the consideration of the housekeepers, I am,

Cordially Yours,

Mrs. Martha M. Williams.

We may live without poetry, music, and art;
We may live without conscience and live without heart;
We may live without friends, we may live without books,
But civilized man cannot live without cooks.
—Owen Meredith.

BREAD

Bread is said to be the staff of life, and is certainly the most essential article of food that the housewife prepares. Therefore it is necessary that the making of it receive the most careful attention. First, that whatever kind of bread is used most in the family be prepared without regard to time or trouble, as in not doing this, poor bread is sure to be the result. It is better to use several kinds of bread, and it is no more trouble to make one kind of bread than another. Most people tire of one kind of bread set before them from one week to another, and in taking from the following recipes for bread, we would ask you to follow the directions explicitly and you will certainly be pleased with the results.

HOME MADE YEAST.

3 Large Potatoes,
1 Large Cup of White Sugar,
2 Heaping Tablespoons of Salt,
1 Tablespoon of Flour,
1 Cup of Yeast,
2 Quarts of Water.
1 Teaspoon of Ginger.

DIRECTIONS—Grate the potatoes; add the salt and sugar, flour and ginger, add one cup of cold water. Beat smooth, then have the two quarts boiling hot and pour on, stirring all the time. It will look about like cooked starch. When about cold add the cup of yeast, set in a warm place to rise; when light, if preferred, can work enough meal into it to mold out in cakes. It will keep some time in a cool place.

POTATO SPONGE FOR BREAD

Pare three good sized potatoes; they must be good mealy potatoes, for soggy ones will not make sponge fit for bread. Put them in a kettle and when done mash them and leave them in the water, having not more than a quart of water to cook them in; pass through a colander, put in the kettle again and heat; when hot pour over about one pint of flour and beat up well; after it cools pour in one quart of lukewarm water and one cup of yeast after it has been soaked well; one good sized cake will be enough; one teaspoon of salt and one teaspoon of sugar, one-half teaspoon of ground ginger, enough flour to make a stiff batter, keep in a warm place to rise. This amount will make six good loaves of bread.

YEAST BREAD NO. 1.

Use a large wooden bowl for making any kind of light bread, make a place in the center after sifting the flour in lightly, add one heaping spoonful of salt, one of sugar and a small pinch of soda so as to insure no sour taste to your bread, add one quart of warm (not hot) water or milk, if milk is used it must be perfectly sweet, and a lump of lard the size of an egg; mix this well together and add one pint of good sponge, make it into soft dough and let rise till very light; then work in enough flour to make the dough rather stiff; knead for at least fifteen minutes and let rise again, when it is light this time make into small loaves and handle as little as possible; grease over the top with butter, and let rise till light and bake in a quick oven, just so it is not hot enough to burn the bread; bake for three-quarters of an hour.

YEAST BREAD NO. 2.

Take a mixing bowl and put what flour is needed to make the necessary amount that is wanted; make a hole in the center and put in your salt, about one teaspoon is needed for four good sized loaves; pour in about one pint of boiling water and stir with a spoon well to keep it from lumping; add cold water to cool about lukewarm, then add your yeast, one cup of yeast sponge will be enough for that amount of bread; cover over with flour and let rise light, then mix in enough flour to make a stiff dough; knead about ten minutes then mold into loaves and let rise again and bake in a rather quick oven; before sending to the oven grease all over the top with butter and again when removed from the oven.

GRANDMOTHER'S SALT RISING BREAD.

One pint of water just as warm as the hand can bear; one teaspoon of salt, one heaping teaspoon of sugar; mix this together; stir in as much flour as is needed to make it the same as pancake dough; set this bowl in hot water, as hot as the water first used; let it remain in the water, keeping it the same heat at least three hours, then thicken with flour again the same as it first was, for this rising will become thin in rising; it will be necessary usually for it to stand again as long as at first; sometimes it will rise more rapidly than others; when ready to put in the mixing bowl scald one cup of flour and let it cool; mix the rising with it and water, add one teaspoon more of salt and a pinch of soda-dissolved in the warm water; make into a stiff dough and knead at least one-half an hour; make into loaves and let rise until light and bake in a moderate oven for one hour.

NO. 1 SALT RISING BREAD THAT NEVER FAILS.

Use two large tablespoons of meal, one-half teaspoon of salt, one teaspoon of sugar, one-half cup of sweet milk, set the milk on the stove and let it come to the boiling point; scald the meal and sugar and salt with this, then let it set to rise till morning, then take one teaspoon of sugar, one of salt and one-half teaspoon of soda; scald these with one pint of hot water; after scalding cool with cold water till about lukewarm; add the rising that was made to rise over night and thicken with flour that has been set in the oven till it is warm; add flour until it is a rather stiff batter; set in a kettle of hot water, as hot as you can bear your hand in comfortably; keep the water the same temperature; when light add about one tablespoon of sweet lard and as much flour as will make a stiff dough; mold into loaves and let rise till light and bake in a moderate oven. This bread is very white, and if kneaded enough will, when cut, resemble cake, it is so white.

GOOD CREAM OF TARTAR BISCUITS.

1 Pint of Sweet Milk,
1 Small Cup of Lard or Butter,
1 Teaspoon of Soda,
2 Teaspoons of Cream of Tartar,
3 Pints of Flour,
1 Teaspoon of Salt.

DIRECTIONS—Sift one pint of flour with the cream of tartar two or three times; then sift the remainder of the flour into a mixing bowl; make a hole in the center; add the flour that has the cream of tartar in, and put in lard and salt and soda dissolved in a little warm water; mix well; add the milk by degrees until all is used. Do not knead more than necessary; roll out about one inch thick, cut and bake in a moderate oven. These will be found very light.

LAZY BISCUITS.

6 Cups of Flour,
¾ Cup of Lard,
1 Teaspoon of Salt,
1½ Cup of Cold Water.

DIRECTIONS—Sift the flour and mix the lard thoroughly with it and add the salt and the water by degrees; mix as little as possible. It will look ragged but do not knead; roll and cut with a biscuit cutter and bake in a quick oven. They are nice when properly made.

EXCELLENT BAKING POWDER BISCUITS.

1 Quart of Flour,
3 Teaspoons of Baking Powder,
1 Teaspoon of Salt,
⅔ Cup of Lard and Butter,
1 Cup of Sweet Milk.

DIRECTIONS—Sift flour and baking powder together three times, also have the salt sifted in; have the butter and lard in equal parts and rub with the flour till it is well mixed; add the milk and make a soft dough; roll, cut, and bake in a quick oven. Any biscuit is nicer to roll the dough rather thin then turn together and roll slightly again, then cut out and bake.

FRIED CORN BREAD.

Cut medium sized pieces of corn bread that is cold, if a little stale is better; put some butter in the frying pan and let it get hot; dip the bread in sweet milk or beaten egg, and fry till brown. Mashed apples, sweetened and put on top of the bread before sending to the table is an addition.

CREAM BISCUITS.

1 Pint of Sifted flour,
1 Cup of Cream,
1 Teaspoon of Salt,
2 Teaspoons of Baking Powder,
1 Teaspoon of Sugar,
1 Egg.

DIRECTIONS—Sift the flour and baking powders together; add the salt and sugar and the white of the egg beaten well; mix all well with a knife. Do not knead the dough much; roll and cut in small cakes; put in the oven and bake quickly.

GRAHAM BREAD.

4 Cups of Graham Flour,
1 Cup of Corn Meal,
⅔ Cups of Molasses,
1 Teaspoon of Salt,
1 Tablespoon of Butter,
3 Pints of Warm Water,
1 Teapoon of Soda.

DIRECTIONS—Sift corn meal and graham flour together; pour over this the water, and stir well together; add the molasses, butter and salt; dissolve soda in a little warm water; beat well and pour in a deep pan and bake slowly, and at least two hours. This bread is excellent.

LIGHT CORN BREAD.

1 Quart of Meal,
1 Cup of Flour,
½ Cup of Soft Yeast,
1 Teaspoon of Salt,
4 Tablespoons of Sugar,
½ Teaspoon of Soda.

DIRECTIONS—Sift flour and meal together, add the salt and sugar, next the yeast, and warm water enough to make a stiff batter; set to rise over night; add soda in the morning; mold with the hands into a deep pan in small loaves and set to rise again until light; wash over the top with milk; bake in a moderately warm oven until done; then remove and cover over for several minutes.

RUSKS FOR BREAKFAST.

½ Pint of Milk,
1 Teaspoon of Salt,
2 Eggs, ½ Tea Cup of Yeast,
¼ Pound Butter,
½ Pound Sugar,
3 Pints of Flour,
1 Small Teaspoon of Soda.

DIRECTIONS—Warm the milk and add the salt, beaten yolks of the eggs and the two pints of flour and yeast and let rise over night. In the morning cream the butter with the sugar; add the beaten whites of the eggs and the soda dissolved in a little warm water; mix into the sponge thoroughly with the hands; also mix the remaining pint of flour and set to rise; when light mold into rolls and put in a pan; when light prick with a fork and bake in a rather quick oven.

RICE GEMS.

Take one pint of rice cooked very tender, one cup of flour, a small piece of butter, one teaspoon of salt, one egg beaten light, one cup of sweet milk, one-half teaspoon of soda and one teaspoon of cream of tartar; sift the cream of tartar in the cup of flour and soda dissolved in warm water. Bake in gem pans.

BUCKWHEAT CAKES.

Take one quart of warm (not hot) water, one-half cup of soft yeast, two large tablespoons of molasses and two tablespoons of salt; mix with enough buckwheat flour to make a thick batter; set in a warm place to rise over night; next morning stir in a teaspoon of soda dissolved in a tablespoon of hot water; stir this in on beginning breakfast, and let set at least a half hour in a warm place. When baked these cakes are delicious. Buckwheat cakes are fit to eat only just as they come from the griddle.

TEA MUFFINS.

Use one quart of flour, two heaping teaspoons of baking powder, sifted three times, two eggs well beaten, one tablespoon of melted butter, two cups of sweet milk, one teaspoon of sugar; Mix well and bake in muffin rings in a quick oven.

APPLE PANCAKE.

Take pan cake dough, or any light dough: have the apples chopped fine; to one quart of dough add about one large cup of the apples, one cup of white sugar, if the apples are sour; stir the dough each time any is put on the griddle. Bake quick and rather thin.

CORN MUFFINS.

One-half pint of flour, one pint of corn meal, one tablespoon of butter, one tablespoon of sugar; melt the butter; add two eggs and enough sweet milk to make a rather thin batter, one teaspoon of cream of tartar, sifted in the flour, and one-half teaspoon of soda dissolved in hot water. Bake in muffin rings in a quick oven.

YEAST MUFFINS.

Take a piece of light dough after it has been raised the second time; work in two tablespoons of butter, one-half cup of sugar, two eggs; add a teaspoon of salt and work all of this in the dough and put a small piece of dough in each muffin ring and let rise till very light and bake in a quick oven.

WHITE HOUSE ROLLS.

1 Small Cup of Yeast,
1 Tablespoon of Sugar,
1 Small Piece of Lard.
1 Large Cup of Milk.
1 Teaspoon of Salt.

DIRECTIONS—Warm the milk slightly, (it must be sweet milk); put enough flour in the mixing bowl and add the sugar, salt and lard. Do not put in a piece of lard larger than an egg; then add the yeast and milk; and mix rather soft; let rise till very light. Now make stiff and let rise again; then mold with the hands and put in tins and raise till very light. Bake in a quick oven.

PULLED BREAD.

Take any kind of light bread after it is baked; while it is warm pull it to pieces, about as large as a biscuits; put back in the oven and brown nicely and eat warm with butter and thin slices of cheese and celery.

BOSTON BROWN BREAD.

3 Cups of Corn Meal,
2 Cups of Graham Flour,
1 Heaping Teaspoon of Soda,
1 Teaspoon of Salt.
½ Cup of Molasses.
1 Cup of Cold Water.

DIRECTIONS—Sift meal and Graham together; add molasses and water, and soda dissolved in a little hot water; then the salt; and mix well. Butter a pan; set in a steamer and steam five hours; then set in the oven about twenty minutes, or long enough to brown slightly.

GRAHAM GEMS.

1½ Cup of Sour Milk,
1 Tablespoon of White Sugar,
1 Teaspoon of Soda,
3 Cups of Graham Flour,
1 Teaspoon of Salt,
1 Egg.

DIRECTIONS—Put the milk in a pan, and add the egg after it has been beaten; add sugar, salt and soda next; sift the Graham in. It will seem a little stiff, but must not add any more milk. Have gem tins very hot, and bake in a quick oven.

DELICIOUS MUFFINS.

1 Large Tablespoon of Butter,
5 Eggs,
1 Quart of Sweet Milk,
1 Quart of Flour,
1 Teaspoon of Salt,
1 Tablespoon of Sugar.

DIRECTIONS—Beat the eggs separately; add the butter to the yolks; beat well, then add milk and flour alternately; then add the salt and sugar, and whites of eggs whipped in lightly. Have the pan hot and greased slightly. Have the oven hot and bake quickly. Eat immediately, after done.

CORN FRITTERS.

½ Cup of Milk,
1 Cup of Flour,
1 Teaspoon of Salt,
¼ Teaspoon Pepper,
1 Tablespoon of Melted Butter,
1 Can of Corn.

DIRECTIONS—Beat an egg light and add one-half cup of milk; pour this mixture upon one cup of flour, and beat well; then add one teaspoon of salt, one-fourth teaspoon of pepper, and a tablespoon of melted butter; mix and add one-half can of corn; drop by spoonfuls into boiling lard. Cook three minutes.

OAT MEAL CAKES.

Use a quart of cooked oat meal; take enough warm water to moisten it; add about one pint of sour milk, and one teaspoon heaping full of soda dissolved in warm water; add two eggs beaten light, two large cups of flour, to make them more easily turned; add one teaspoon of salt. They are very nice, and a change from the other kinds of bread for breakfast.

GRAHAM PANCAKES.

Two cups of Graham flour, and one of wheat flour; sift these together; then add enough sour milk to make an ordinary batter; whip one egg light, and add; and one teaspoon of salt, one teaspoon of soda, first dissolved in warm water; mix all well together, and bake on a hot griddle and serve immediately with butter and syrup.

LIGHT MUFFINS.

1 Pint of Flour,
½ Teaspoon of Salt,
2 Ounces of Butter,
½ Cup of Yeast,
1 Large Cup Sweet Milk,
2 Eggs.

DIRECTIONS—Sift the flour; rub butter and flour together; add salt, yeast and eggs. Beat eggs separately, until very light; stir in the milk last, having it slightly warm; beat and set to rise. Let raise until very light. Bake in muffin rings.

KENTUCKY DODGERS.

2 Cups of Sour Cream,
1 Cup of Sweet Milk,
1 Egg,
2 Teaspoons of Butter,
1 Teaspoon of salt,
2 Small Teaspoons of Soda.

DIRECTIONS—Sift the meal and beat the eggs well; dissolve the soda in sour cream; add the sweet milk to this, also the salt and butter; stir enough meal in so that a spoonful will keep in shape without spreading in the pan. Bake in a quick oven until a rich brown. Serve very hot.

OLD FASHIONED CORN CAKE.

1 Egg,
1 Small Teaspoon of Soda,
2 Cups of Sour Milk.
2 Cups of Meal,
½ Teacup of Flour,
½ Teaspoon of Salt.

DIRECTIONS—Sift the meal and beat the eggs until very light; dissolve soda in the milk; mix flour with the meal and sift in lightly; add egg and salt. The batter will be thin. Put two small spoonfuls in a cake, and bake quick; to be eaten while warm. The cakes must not be thicker than one-eighth of an inch.

GRAHAM WAFERS.

1 Teaspoon of Salt,
½ Pound of Graham Flour,
½ Pint of Sweet Cream,
1 Teaspoon of Sugar.

DIRECTIONS—Mix quickly and thoroughly; roll and cut as thin as possible; cut in strips; prick and bake in a quick oven.

CREAM CRACKERS.

1 Quart of Flour,
¼ Teaspoon of Salt,
2 Tablespoons of Sugar,
1 Teaspoon of Baking Powder,
4 Tablespoons of Butter,
3 Eggs, Whites Only.

DIRECTIONS—Sift flour and baking powder and put in a mixing bowl; add butter and eggs, after beating them light; add the salt; make up stiff, and knead rapidly; roll and cut. Cut with a square cutter; drop in a kettle of boiling water for five minutes; skim out and put in a colander to drain; then put them in a greased tin and bake in a hot oven, but do not let them brown too much.

LIGHT CRACKERS.

½ Pint of Light Dough,
¼ Cup of Butter.

DIRECTIONS—Add butter to the dough, and mix well together; divide the dough into several parts; roll thin and cut in squares; prick with a fork; let rise again and bake a pale brown.

TOMATO TOAST.

Toast bread and lay on a platter, and stew some tomatoes till well done, and season with pepper and salt; when done add cream with a little flour; let it cook, then pour over the slices of toast, and serve at once.

GERMAN TOAST.

Cut five hard boiled eggs in thin slices; put a piece of butter the size of an egg in a sauce pan; when hot add some finely chopped onion; cook till tender, but do not let it brown; then add a little flour, and a cup of milk; let cook till it thickens then pour over the toast and put the slices of the eggs around and serve.

FRENCH TOAST.

½ Dozen Slices of Stale Bread,
2 Eggs,
1 Cup of Cream,
1 Cup of Lard,
1 Pinch of Salt and Pepper.

DIRECTIONS—First dip in the cream, then in the beaten egg; have the lard hot; put in a sufficient number of slices that will be easily managed, for if crowded it will be sure not to brown. When brown on both sides, put on a hot plate and serve at once. Sprinkle sugar over, if desired, or some good jell. Put over in thin slices.

HAM ON TOAST.

Boil the ham until very tender, then chop fine and add two well beaten eggs, some butter and a little pepper and salt; put in a sauce pan and cook till it thickens; then pour over the toast. Serve hot.

BIRDS ON TOAST.

Cook the birds till very tender; bake them till nice brown; cut in pieces and put on the slices of toast; make a gravy and pour over. Serve at once.

BUTTERED TOAST.

Toast several slices of stale bread; first dip in warm (not hot) water; lay on a platter and butter it well, and cover over and set in the oven a few moments, and serve while very hot.

CREAM TOAST.

Toast any number of slices of bread desired; have ready a dressing prepared as follows: Take one cup of milk and one of cream, a piece of butter the size of an egg; salt slightly; heat it almost to a boiling point and pour over the toast in a deep dish. Keep covered till ready to serve.

CHEESE TOAST.

Toast some slices of bread and butter them; grate some cheese over; put a spoonful of cheese to each slice of bread; set in the oven and let remain a few minutes. Serve while hot.

TOMATOES ON TOAST.

Use only very ripe tomatoes; after removing the peel mash and press through a colander; put in a pan and season as usual; cook fifteen minutes; take some stale slices of bread and toast a golden brown, and place on a platter; butter each slice; pour over the mixture and send to the table immediately.

JOHNNY CAKE.

1 Cup of Sour Milk,
½ Teaspoon of Salt,
½ Teaspoon of Soda,
1 Tablespoon of Butter,
2 Eggs,
½ Cup of Flour,
¼ Cup of Sugar,
1 Cup of Corn Meal.

DIRECTIONS—Sift flour, salt, sugar and meal together, and rub the butter through them; then beat the eggs; add the milk, after dissolving the soda in the milk; mix well and bake in a shallow tin; cut with a knife dipped in hot water or laid on a stove until hot.

TO MAKE NICE BUNS.

1 Cup of Milk,
1 Cup of Sugar,
¾ Cup of Yeast,
½ Cup of Butter.

DIRECTIONS—Mix all the ingredients together and make a stiff dough at night; in the morning add the butter, let rise again and mold and cut with a cutter, and put in a pan and let rise again. When very light bake in a moderate oven and on removing from oven, brush over with milk and sugar.

RECIPE FOR BAKING POWDERS.

¼ Pound of Tartaric Acid,
¼ Pound of Soda,
1 Pint of Flour.

Sift all together six times; then put in cans and keep air tight. This is a good baking powder, and will keep a long time.

MEATS.

TO BOIL HAM.

A ham weighing ten or twelve pounds will require to be soaked at least twelve hours; then remove and put in a kettle, and pour enough boiling water to cover it; add some vinegar, about one-half cup to a ham of that size; boil steadily for about three hours. Try with a fork to ascertain if well done, as some are more tender than others; remove from the water in which it has been cooked, after it is cold, as it makes any kind of meat more firm to cool in the liquor in which they have been cooked.

TO BAKE A HAM.

Choose a ham weighing not more than eight pounds; make a plain crust; roll, cut and put the ham in, just the same as you would make dumplings; fold the crust over and put in a pan; set in the oven and bake one hour for every pound of ham; cover over close when baking. When done remove the crust and sprinkle with sugar and melted butter together; set in the oven and bake one hour slowly; then take up and put in something that a cover can be put on, and put a weight over it. When cold it will cut in nice slices.

TO COOK VENISON HAM.

After trimming the ham nicely, put in a baking pan; put thin slices of bacon over it, and some slices of onions, and some spices and thyme. A cup of good wine added to the water in which it is cooked improves it, and it cooks more easily. The wine must be sour. Cover closely, and when nearly done remove the cover and let it brown slightly and it will be ready to serve. For a common sized ham it will take from two to two and a half hours to cook. Serve with the gravy put around it, also the onions.

PORK CROQUETTES.

1 Pint of Meat,
1 Tablespoon Butter,
2 Eggs,
1 Onion,
½ Cup of Bread Crumbs,
½ Tablespoon of Salt,
¼ Teaspoon of Pepper,
1 Teacup Hot Water.

DIRECTIONS—Chop meat fine; add melted butter; next the bread crumbs and beaten eggs, salt and onions chopped fine; add the water and cook till all is well mixed; then pour into a pan to cool them; roll into balls; dip in egg and then in crackers. Fry a good brown.

BEEF STEAK FINGERS.

2 Pounds of Steak,
1 Pint of Hot Water,
1 Egg,
1 Onion,
1 Teaspoon of Salt,
½ Teaspoon of Pepper,
3 Crackers.

DIRECTIONS—Pound the steak and put in a frying pan and cover with the water, add salt and pepper and cook slowly for an hour. If the steak is very tender it need not cook so long; when done remove and have the egg beaten; cut in slices and dip in the egg, then in crackers, after rolling them fine; fry in hot fat until nicely browned. Nice served with mashed potatoes. Make a gravy to be eaten with it. Nice with lemons sliced thin to garnish with.

VEAL LOAF.

3 Pounds of Veal,
2 Cups of Bread Crumbs,
1 Small Cup of Meat Broth,
1 Lemon,
¼ Teaspoon of Pepper,
2 Eggs,
¼ Teaspoon of Salt,
¼ Teaspoon of Mace.

DIRECTIONS—Boil the veal tender; chop fine and add the meat broth; then the eggs beaten stiff, and the juice of the lemon; now the mace, pepper and salt; mix well and press into a loaf and put in a bread pan and cover and bake till a nice brown: remove and let cool and slice thin and serve between buttered bread as sandwiches.

PIGS' BRAINS, FRIED.

Brains from 3 Pigs,
1 Teaspoon of Salt,
¼ Teaspoon of Pepper,
1 Egg,
3 Crackers.

DIRECTIONS—Put brains in salt water over night, and when ready to fry, drain well; sprinkle with pepper; roll crackers fine (or use cracker meal); beat the eggs well; first dip the brains in the egg, then in crackers; fry in hot grease until a rich brown. Are very nice to serve with toast for breakfast with tomato sauce.

PIGS' FEET, FRIED.

4 Feet,
1 Egg,
1 Tablespoon of Salt,
4 Crackers.

DIRECTIONS—Cook the feet until well done. They can be kept whole by tying them up in a thin cloth. After they are well done remove from the cloth and split in two pieces; dip in the beaten egg, then in the crackers, after it has been rolled fine; fry in hot grease until brown. Serve with any good sauce that is preferred.

HAMBURG STEAK.

1 Pound of Raw Beef,
1 Small Onion,
1 Small Piece of Beef Suet,
¼ Teaspoon of Pepper,
1 Teaspoon of Salt.

DIRECTIONS—Chop beef, onion and suet very fine and mix with the meat; make into cakes and roll in flour; fry in butter till done, and a delicate brown. Serve with sauce.

TO COOK A ROAST OF MUTTON.

Take five pounds of the leg of a mutton and put in a baking pan; put a small amount of water on and peel some onions and put around the meat; (some prefer carrots or potatoes) put plenty of flour over the meat, also pepper and salt; cover the pan and set it in the oven; cook till well done, then remove to a platter and garnish with the onions and some sprigs of parsley.

VEAL SAUSAGE.

Chop some veal in a chopping bowl, season with sage, salt and pepper and when all is mixed well, make into little cakes and dip in beaten egg and cracker meal and fry a golden brown. These are excellent. If the meat seems too dry add a little warm water.

BEEF LIVER, FRIED.

After washing the liver, cut in slices one-half of an inch thick; put a liberal sized piece of butter and some lard in a frying pan and let it get smoking hot and roll the pieces of liver in powdered crackers; then put in the pan and fry very fast, but do not let it burn. When a nice brown on both sides, put on a platter and cover over and put some thinly sliced onions in the grease and fry till brown and garnish the liver with them. A gravy can be made from some beef drippings and poured over this, or if liked, the gravy can be omitted—is very nice either way.

TO MAKE GOOD SAUSAGE.

Use the tenderloin of a hog, it is much better than beef, as beef is dry and scarcely ever tender; cut in strips and grind very fine; mix by adding salt and pepper, bth black and caynene; add sage to taste. If it seems too dry, add some warm water, but it is better if the meat, after grinding, seems too dry within itself, to make a tea of the pepper instead of putting the dry powder in the meat, and if wanted to keep a considerable length of time, will keep better than putting water alone in. When mixed put in sacks and hang in a dry, cool place

BAKED SAUSAGE.

Make some sausage into cakes and dip into bread crumbs after dipping them in egg; put in a greased pan; set in the oven and cook till well done and serve with cream gravy.

SAUSAGE ROLLS.

Use any good fresh sausage, pork is the best, but must not be too fat; make a puff paste; make the sausage in rolls about three inches long, and one inch around; roll the paste not more than one-third of an inch thick, put the sausage in; roll over and wet the edges of the crust to prevent opening; brush over with sweet milk; put in rather a deep pan and put in the oven and cook till done, and a light brown. These are nice either cold or hot. The addition of some meat jelly to any of the patties or pies is an addition, as they will not seem dry and tasteless, if not used in several days after making, if the weather is cool enough to keep them nicely.

DIRECTIONS FOR THE JELLY—Put beef or any kind of meat bones on with enough hot water and cook for several hours; let cool and you will have a nice jelly and is no trouble, as it needs no attention, only to put it on to cook.

TO STEW LIVER.

Cut in rather thick slices and put in salt water for two hours before putting on to cook; then cook till it is very tender and serve with any good gravy that is liked.

TO FRY LIVER AS CUTLETS.

Allow two eggs to every pound of liver; cut the liver thin and scald it, let drain, or if needed immediately, wipe dry with a cloth; salt it, and beat eggs well, and dip each piece in the egg and then in powdered cracker, or meal is very nice. Fry till brown. Serve with tomato sauce.

PORK CHOPS.

Trim, and have them about an inch thick; salt and put in a frying pan with some fat, and fry a nice brown, and till they are well done; put on a platter, and chop some onion fine; add some sage and pepper; let cook a few minutes in the gravy and pour around the chops.

HOW TO UTILIZE COLD MEATS.

Cold meat of any kind; put in a kettle and cook thoroughly done, in as little water as not to let it burn; let it cool, keeping it covered closely while cooling; after it is cold put in a chopping bowl and chop fine and season with salt, pepper, and a little sage, if liked; put in a crock and cover over and put a weight on, and the next day it will be ready to slice; have the slices about one-fourth of an inch thick; dip in a beaten egg, then cracker meal, and fry in hot grease till a nice brown and serve with baked apples.

TO BAKE A HEART.

Take a beef heart and do not wash it, but dry with a cloth; make a stuffing of bread crumbs, sage, some butter, pepper and salt; mix and moisten with water enough to make it the right consistency; then fill the cavities of the heart; bake with enough water in the pan to baste it with. It will require about three hours for a common sized heart to bake tender. Make a gravy and pour around the heart on a platter. Serve with any good tart jell.

PORK.

The sirloin of pork for chops and roasts; the hind leg for roasts and smoked hams; the fore loin is used for second choice roasts and chops; the back furnishes inferior roasts and for boiling, also is used for corning; the shoulder is used mostly for pickling and smoking; the head is used to make head cheese and mince meat; the feet mostly for pickling.

BEEF.

The fore ribs makes a very nice roast, and the middle ribs also; choose the brisket pieces for soups. The neck makes nice soup, and is used for mince meat and sausage; shoulder is used for roasts, stews and hash. The hind quarter contains the porter house and sirloin steak, also the finest roasts is taken from the hind quarters of the beef. Different parts of it is used for stews, hash and soups; the thick part of the flank for corned beef; the veiney part for dried beef; the thin part of the flank for corned beef and boiling. The tongue is used boiled, fresh, smoked or pickled. The heart is very nice stuffed and baked. The liver is sometimes fried; and suet makes a nice pie crust and is used in pudding and mince meat.

MUTTON.

The loin is used for roasting and chops. The leg is mostly used for chops, sometimes for boiling; the loin second choice for chops; the loin rump end for boiling and roasts. Breast is used for stews. Mutton is best from sheep not too old, three years old makes the nicest meat, but if fat some older will do. Very young sheep do not make as good flavored meat, as it seems tasteless and is flabby.

BOILED PIGS' FEET, PICKLED.

Clean and scrape the feet well, enclose each one in a thin muslin cloth and put in boiling water; salt it not quite as salt as you would other meat; when done put in vinegar, and after remaining several days they will be ready for use. Do not have the vinegar too strong as it will spoil them. If the vinegar is very strong dilute it some with water before putting the feet in.

BOILED TONGUE.

The tongue should be soaked in weak salt water for several hours previous to cooking; then cook till very tender; after removing from the stove, put in cold water and the outer skin can easily be removed; lay on a platter, and with a sharp knife gash across in checks or diamonds. Serve with veal jelly.

TO MAKE GOOD MEAT JELLY.

The shank bones of beef are best for making this jelly; put to cook in a liberal amount of water and cook till thoroughly done; remove the meat and strain the liquor into a flat pan and when cold will cut like any other jell. Is nice for cold meats. Chicken can be cooked in the same way and jelly obtained from it also. Salt and pepper the meat while cooking.

BROILING

To broil any kind of meat it is necessary to have a very hot fire, or plenty of live coals at least, and a good gridiron is indispensible and should be kept scrupuously clean; have the iron well greased, and very hot before putting the meat on; turn it frequently, but do not stick a fork in the meat while broiling, as this causes the juice to leave the meat. Some dip the meat in melted fat before putting on to broil, but this is not necessary. Do not salt and pepper the meat till it is cooked. Serve this hot, on hot plates.

TO BOIL MUTTON.

Choose a rather lean piece to boil, as mutton is not good if very fat; put to boil in soft water, slightly salted, but do not put as much salt in at first as is needed to season the meat, as this prevents meat from cooking in as short a time as it will to wait till it is half done at least. Cook till very tender; remove and keep covered till it is thoroughly cold.

TO COOK SPARE RIBS.

After the ribs have been cracked across and cut apart, leaving not more than two ribs together; salt and rub some flour and butter together and put the ribs in a baking pan; baste with the butter and flour and keep covered closely, and do not put only about one-half pint of water over them when putting in to bake; baste often with the flour and butter while cooking, as this will insure a nicely cooked spare rib.

A GOOD MINT SAUCE.

Take any amount of green mint required and chop till very fine; then add some sugar and good cider vinegar; let it stand several days and it is ready for use. It is used with meats, and is preferred by some to any other sauce with mutton.

TO BROIL HAM.

Cut in rather thick slices and remove all the fat; have the fire very hot and put your ham over to broil; turn often and when done sufficiently lay on a platter and put a liberal piece of butter on each piece of ham. Serve at once.

TO FRY PORK IN BATTER.

Cut the meat in slices and salt and pepper it; make a batter as for pancakes; dip each slice of meat in the batter, then in cracker crumbs; fry in very hot grease till well done. Serve with tomato sauce or chopped pickles, or mustard if preferred.

PIGS' FEET CHEESE.

Cook the feet till very tender; remove all of the bones and season with salt and pepper, and a small amount of allspice; pack in a crock and put a heavy weight on; let remain several days before using. Serve sliced in vinegar.

TO FRY FROG LEGS.

Cover the legs with boiling water; then after remaining in the water for half an hour remove to cold water and let them remain in this for a few minutes; then put a spider on and put in a piece of butter and let it get hot; put the legs in after dipping them in flour; fry until a crisp brown; arrange them nicely in a dish and garnish with slices of tomatoes fried in butter and some small squares of toast on the slices of tomatoes.

TO ROAST BEEF.

Take any amount of beef that is required and salt and pepper it and dredge well with flour; put in a baking pan and set in the oven and cover closely; do not put very much water in at a time; baste often and only add water as it is needed; when well done take upon a platter and garnish with cranberry sauce, put around it by spoonfuls a little ways apart. It looks very pretty if pickles is preferred to garnish with; slice them very thin and put around the meat. Any kind of gravy can be used to serve with roast beef that is preferred.

TO FRY HAM.

If the ham is smoked slice it about one-fourth of an inch thick; have a skillet ready and moderately hot; put in enough grease to keep the ham from sticking; then put in and fry very slow until the meet is cooked sufficient; then fry fast till it browns nicely; remove to a platter and pour some cream in the grease and pour over the meat and serve.

TO FRY BEEF STEAK, NO. 1.

Choose porter house steak if a nice, tender steak is wanted; pound or chop it well; have a frying pan ready with some butter in it, and have it smoking hot. Before putting the steak in salt and pepper it and fry very fast; then take up and put some butter over each piece of steak; cover closely for a few minutes —keeping the platter in a warm place, and it is ready to serve.

ANOTHER WAY TO FRY STEAK.

Pound the beef as in No. 1. and pepper and salt it; dip in flour or powdered cracker; have the pan with a little more butter in than for the other way; heat it till very hot and put the steak in and cover; fry fast till a crisp brown; put on a platter; make a brown gravy and pour over the steak. Serve with tomato sauce.

POULTRY AND GAME

TO KILL A FOWL.

The best way is to hang them up, and cut off the head, as in this way they bleed more freely. The best way to pick a fowl is to remove the feathers without scalding. A turkey, duck or goose should never be scalded. Pick carefully so as not to break the skin. To draw the crop split the skin of all poultry on the back of the neck when wished to be dressed whole. After splitting the skin pull the neck upwards, cut the neck off close to the body, leaving a skewer in the back of the neck after the dressing has been put in. In drawing the entrails be very careful not to break the gall, as it is very hard to wash off. Cut the gizzard open and remove the inner skin and wash it well. Some good cooks prefer not to put any water on poultry, but dry all the blood off on a cloth, but properly cooked, this part is immaterial as to how it is done. Any kind of a fowl should not lay in water very long or it will make it tasteless, but some dark meat is improved somewhat by treating in this way, but do not let it remain in water too long.

CHICKEN CROQUETTES.

2 Cups of Chopped Meat, Chicken or Turkey,
¼ Cup of Melted Butter,
½ Pint of Sweet Cream,
3 Tablespoons of Good Wine,
A Very Little Nutmeg,
3 Tablespoons of Flour,
A Little Salt and Pepper,
Juice of One-half a Lemon,
¼ Pint of Chicken Soup,
¼ Pint of Mashed Potatoes.
1 Cup of Rolled Crackers.

Directions—Chop the chicken and add salt, pepper, nutmeg and lemon juice and the wine last; put the cream, flour and butter in a sauce pan and cook till it thickens; pour over the other on a platter and let cool; whip an egg; roll and cut in cone shapes; dip in egg then in the rolled crackers; cook in boiling lard, a few at a time. They are very nice.

CHICKEN A La CREME.

Clean and wash a nice fat chicken and cut it up nicely; stew very tender, then make a thickening of cream and flour, seasoned with pepper, salt and butter; have ready two cakes made from pie crust, rolled thin and cut in squares and baked; lay the crusts on a dish and put the chicken and gravy over them. Serve while hot.

ESCALOPED CHICKEN.

1 Chicken,
1 Dozen Crackers,
¼ Cup Butter,
½ Cup of Sweet Cream,
1 Teaspoon of Salt,
1 Pinch of Pepper,
½ Dozen fresh Oysters,
1 Teaspoon of Lemon Juice.

DIRECTIONS—Salt and boil the chicken very tender and remove from the bone and chop the meat; butter a baking dish and put a layer of the chopped chicken in the bottom, then some bits of butter, and moisten with cream; then a layer of chicken and a few drops of lemon juice, and crackers and chicken next. Put crackers and butter on top and bake in a hot oven.

BARBECUED RABBIT.

Take a nice, fat rabbit and grease well; rub with butter, pepper and salt; lay on a gridiron; turn often till well done, then remove to a pan with plenty of butter; set in a hot oven for a few minutes. Serve with the following sauce:

DIRECTIONS FOR SAUCE—

3 Tablespoons of Vinegar,
1 Teaspoon of Mustard,
2 Tablespoons of Jelly,
1 Tablespoonful of Lemon Juice.

Mix these well together and pour over the rabbit and serve.

FRIED CHICKEN.

Choose a medium sized chicken after it has been nicely dressed; lay in salt water for an hour, then wipe dry and have the grease hot; roll in flour and fry slowly until a rich brown and lay on a platter and serve. Garnish with small potato balls.

BROILED PRAIRIE CHICKEN.

Prepare for cooking and put in a steamer; set over hot water until tender; rub with salt and pepper; lay on a gridiron over good bright coals. When a nice brown take up and cover with melted butter and set in a hot oven for a few minutes. Serve with currant jelly.

PARTRIDGE FRICASSEE.

Prepare as if you were going to boil them; put in a sauce pan and cover with hot water and cook until tender. Thicken the gravy with a little flour and some butter rubbed into it; season to taste with some pepper and salt; toast some slices of bread very nice; put on a hot dish and pour the fricassee over and serve very hot. This is a very nice dish.

BAKED PARTRIDGES.

Split the birds in the back; take a can of fresh oysters; make a dressing with the oysters and bread crumbs, some butter and sage; fill in and sew the bird up; fill as many as needed and put in a baking pan with a little hot water and butter; cook until well done. Serve with mushroom sauce. Garnish with slices of lemon.

LARDED RABBIT.

Cut the ribs from the rabbit and put in a baking pan; cut thin slices of bacon; bake until very tender; put on a platter and serve with brown sauce.

CHAUD FROID CHICKEN.

1 Roasted Chicken,
2 Tablespoons of Butter,
1 Tablespoon of Flour,
1 Pint of milk,
1 Teaspoon of Salt,
¼ Teaspoon of Pepper.

DIRECTIONS—Roast the chicken tender and remove the skin; cut in nice pieces; put a pan on and melt the butter; add flour, salt and pepper, then the milk; boil until it thickens and pour over the chicken. Garnish with parsley.

STUFFED QUAILS

4 Birds,
1 Quart of Water,
3 Cups of Bread Crumbs,
½ Cup of Sweet Cream,
2 Tablespoons of Butter,
1 Pinch of Salt and Pepper.

DIRECTIONS—Choose nice fat quails and sprinkle a little salt in each. For the stuffing use the butter and bread crumbs; cream salt and pepper, and mix all well together; stuff the birds well and fasten down the legs; put in a baking pan and dredge each one in flour; cut some butter over them; add the water and cook in a hot oven till well done; baste often. After removing from oven lay on a platter and put some gravy over them.

TO ROAST TURKEY

After picking and drawing the turkey, put it in a steamer or anything it can be cooked in. A patent cooker is good, as they can be steamed until done; then remove and bake in the oven; have the dressing ready and fill and put in the pan around the turkey. A nice dressing can be made as follows: Take equal parts of bread crumbs and crackers; mix with some of the broth from the turkey and one whole egg; season with sage, thyme, pepper and salt. Some like oysters added, but it is quite nice without. Do not have the dressing made too dry, that spoils the taste as well as looks of any dressing. Serve with cranberry sauce.

CURRIED CHICKEN.

Roast a young chicken till very tender and cut in pieces; put three tablespoons of butter and one tablespoon of curry powder in a skillet; and one large onion; chop fine and let it brown slightly; then add one tablespoon of flour and stir well; add one cup of chicken broth, and one-half cup of sweet milk; season with pepper and salt, if it is not quite salt enough; cook till it thickens, then put the chicken on a platter and pour this around it. Serve at once.

TO ROAST A GOOSE.

After preparing to cook, make a dressing as usual; season with salt, pepper, some sage and butter, one egg and enough water to make the quantity desired damp enough; proceed to fill the goose, and fasten by using a strong thread or twine; put in a roaster and bake two hours, if not too old, but if it is, will require about three hours to bake. Do not put in any more water than is needed, if it is covered closely it will not require much water to bake it. Serve with mashed potatoes made in balls, and melted butter poured over them, and set in the oven till they are a nice brown; put them around the goose on the platter on which it is served; and make a gravy to serve with it also. A goose baked in this way is excellent.

TO BROIL BIRDS.

First after dressing them split them open in the back and let them lay awhile in salt water; melt some butter in a pan and wipe the birds dry with a cloth; dip them in melted butter; then lay on a gridiron over a clear fire; after browning on one side turn and have both sides a golden brown; put on plates and put some small pieces of butter over them and pepper; cover closely and set in the oven a few minutes, then they are ready to serve.

CHICKEN JELLY.

Dress and joint a good sized chicken and put to cook with half gallon of cold water; season; remove all the fat and cook slowly till only one pint remains; press through a colander and if any fat appears skim it off. Serve cold. The chicken must be young, if not more water will have to be added in order to cook it sufficiently. This jelly is often used to garnish meats with, and is very nice.

Fish and Oysters

TO BROIL FISH.

Fish is very nice broiled. First, salt the fish that is to be broiled and dip in some oil, which is better for fish than butter; put over the fire and watch them closely, as they brown very easily. They require more attention in broiling than anything else, as if not done thoroughly through are not good. It takes a longer time to broil fish than any other meat. Serve with any sauce that is liked.

FISH FORCE MEAT.

Take one pound of any good fresh fish and remove the bones; pound it well; then add the whites of two eggs, a little at a time; then add one pint of good cream, one teaspoon of salt and a pinch of pepper. Mix well and it is ready for use.

A GOOD WAY TO BOIL FISH.

Clean fish and put in boiling water that has been salted; allow it to boil ten minutes or longer to every pound of fish; after it has been cooked a while add a spoonful of vinegar or lemon juice; (use a teaspoon to measure); when done remove to a platter; pour over some melted butter. Serve at once.

BAKED WHITE FISH.

Clean the fish well and salt and fill with a good dressing; sew the fish up and place in baking pan; allow one and a half pints of hot water to a medium sized fish. Before putting the fish in the oven to bake rub well with flour and bake in a quick oven; requires about one hour if not too large. Serve with tomato sauce.

TROUT ENPAPILLOTES.

Take four trouts and make a stuffing of fish force meat, salt and pepper; have enough water to make the right consistency; have an oiled paper for each fish; take thin slices of fat pork and lay on the pieces of paper and lay the fish on the meat; add a little salt and pepper; then fold the paper over and tie with a cord; cook in a baking pan with a very little water till well done. Do not have the oven too hot. Serve with any sauce desired.

TO BOIL FRESH COD.

Dress the fish and put in cold water salted; let stand a few minutes; put in a kettle and cover with cold water and let cook till well done; put on a fish platter and serve with butter.

TO COOK TROUT.

Cook them with the heads on after being washed, and rub with salt and pepper; fry in butter and lard in equal parts till they are a golden brown. They are very easily cleaned, as they have no scales. They can be boiled and served with any kind of sauce.

STEWED OYSTERS.

1 Can of Best Fresh Oysters,
2 Tablespoons of Butter,
1 Quart of New Milk,
¼ Teaspoon of Pepper,
1 Teaspoon of Salt,
1 Tablespoon of Flour.

DIRECTIONS—Drain the liquor off and put to boil; skim and add the milk, butter and flour; then add to the milk the pepper and salt; put in the oysters and let heat a minute and they are ready to serve.

FISH GRAVY.

As scarcely anyone likes the flavor of fish in gravy, they will find it much improved by pouring about half of the fat out and adding meat fryings or butter; add flour and milk; stir well and boil five minutes; pour over the baked or fried fish.

COD FISH BALLS.

After washing the fish shred fine; put in sweet milk and heat boiling hot; remove from stove and soak three hours; then wash from the milk and add about one-third as much mashed potatoes as you have of the fish; add pepper and some sweet cream; make into balls and dip in egg then in cracker meal; fry in hot lard till a nice brown.

CREAMED FISH.

Use any good white fish and separate it into flakes; make a cream sauce, which is given in the sauces; allow a cup of sauce to every two pounds of the fish; spread a layer of the sauce in a baking dish, then a layer of fish; salt and pepper lightly; add a little chopped parsley and a teaspoon of lemon juice; over this put some more of the sauce and bread crumbs, also a small piece of butter; brown in the oven. Canned salmon may be used in this way.

BOILED TROUT MAITRE D'HOTEL.

5 trouts,
3 tablespoons of melted butter,
1 tablespoon of salt,
¼ tablespoon of pepper.

DIRECTIONS—Wash, drain, cut open in back and pepper and salt; rub well with the butter; put on the broiler and broil ten minutes on one side and turn and cook about the same time on the other, or until they are a nice brown; remove to a platter and serve with the following sauce.

DIRECTIONS FOR SAUCE,—
1 pint of Hollandaise sauce,
1 teaspoon of chopped parsley,
1 tablespoon of butter,
¼ teaspoon of pepper,
¼ teaspoon of nutmeg.

Mix all well together and serve.

LOBSTER CUTLETS.

2 lobsters,
1 teaspoon of salt,
1 teaspoon of spices,
1 tablespoon of butter,
1 tablespoon of flour,
1 pint of stock,
2 Eggs.

DIRECTIONS—Chop the meat of the lobsters fine, after being cooked in water enough to cover them; then season; put the butter and flour in a small pan and add the chopped lobsters and stock the lobsters were cooked in; now the eggs well beaten. Reserve one egg to dip the cutlets in when all is mixed; spread in a shallow pan, and when cold cut into long slices and dip in the egg, then in rolled crackers, and fry in hot lard. They are nice.

BAKED BLUE FISH.

4 pounds of fish,
5 crackers,
⅓ pound of salt pork,
1 tablespoon of salt,
¼ teaspoon of pepper,
1 teaspoon chopped parsley,
2 tablespoons of flour.

DIRECTIONS—Scrape and wash the fish clean; then rub with salt; roll the crackers fine; add the parsley, one tablespoon of the chopped pork, one-half of the pepper and half of the salt, and enough cold water to moisten the whole; put the dressing in the fish and fasten with a skewer; put in a dish and cut gashes across the fish two inches long; cut the remainder of the pork in strips and lay across in the gashes; fill the bottom of the baking pan with hot water; bake one hour, basting every few minutes and dredging each time with flour and a little pepper. The water will have to be renewed often, for only the bottom of the pan must be covered.

SMOTHERED FISH.

Clean the fish—any good tender fish may be used; cut in squares; dredge in flour; lay in a pan and put a good sized lump of butter on each piece; salt and pepper; add a cup of hot water; after it it done remove to a platter; and put about a half cup of good cream, in which has been stirred one tablespoon of flour; cook till It thickens; salt and pepper and pour over the fish. This will be found excellent.

TO BAKE FISH WITHOUT STUFFING.

Cut them open in the back; salt and pepper and lay in a pan; baste often with melted butter and water. Do not have more than a teacup of water in when putting in to bake; bake half an hour in a hot oven.

BAKED SALMON.

1 pound can of salmon,
2 tablespoons of butter,
1 cup of bread crumbs,
2 eggs,
1 lemon,
1 teaspoon of salt,
1 teaspoon of pepper.

DIRECTIONS—Pick the salmon to pieces; mix in the butter, salt, pepper, eggs, bread crumbs and juice of the lemon; mix all together and put in a baking dish and set in the oven and bake till well done; it will require about one hour; then remove from the oven and set the dish in cold water till it loosens, and turn into a tureen and make a sauce to pour over it as follows:

1 small cup of melted butter,
1 cup of the liquor from the salmon.
1 egg,
¼ teaspoon of pepper,
1 small teaspoon of salt,
1 pickle,
1 teaspoon of parsley.

Chop the pickle; beat the egg; then add the liquor from the salmon, and parsley, pepper, butter and salt; put on stove and let it boil; then pour over the salmon and serve.

CLAM CHOWDER.

1 quart of opened clams, or ½ peck in shells,
½ pound of salted pork,
3 medium sized onions,
¼ pound of crackers,
3 tablespoon of butter,
¼ teaspoons of pepper,
1 teaspoon of salt.

DIRECTIONS—After the pork has been cut in thin slices fry crisp and cut in pieces, put some of these in a sauce pan that will hold a half gallon or more; then put in a layer of clams; cover with chopped onions, then a layer of crackers; salt and pepper, and add some of the butter, then another layer, same as before and so on until all is used; then cover with hot water and stew till well done. Serve with bread, butter and pickles.

SOUPS.

SIPPETS FOR SOUPS.

Butter some stale slices of bread and put in a hot oven until thoroughly browned; cut in small squares, and just before serving the soup, add some to each bowl. They are very nice, and preferred by some to crackers.

VEAL SOUP.

Two pints of veal broth, one onion chopped fine, and a cup of stewed tomatoes, a piece of butter, salt and pepper; let boil a few minutes and serve.

MUTTON SOUP.

One quart of mutton broth, one cup of chopped celery, one good sized turnip chopped fine and added to the broth, with one pint of hot water; salt and pepper and let cook till the vegetables are tender; remove and strain and serve immediately.

POTATO SOUP

Pare and slice some nice mealy potatoes; about a half dozen; add one quart of cold water and a chopped onion; boil till very tender; mash them and add one large cup of cream, and one bunch of celery, a lump of butter, and salt and pepper to taste. Chop the celery fine and after adding the cream do not boil, but mer five minutes and it is ready to send to the table.

VEGETABLE SOUP.

One quart vegetables, using turnips, carrots, onions, celery, tomatoes, cabbage and potatoes, put in about one quart of water to cook them in; when tender add one quart of beef stock or broth; then add a little salt and pepper; cook thirty minutes, and serve very hot.

PEA SOUP.

2 cups green peas,
3 quarts of water,
½ lb of lean salt pork,
1 stalk of celery,
1 onion,
1 pinch of pepper.

DIRECTIONS—Put the peas and pork to cook, having the water cold: add the pepper, celery and onion; let cook four hours, when it will look thick and smooth. This is a very nice soup.

CLEAR SOUP.

3 lbs. of beef,
4 quarts of cold water,
1 onion,
1 stalk of celery,
1 teaspoon of pepper,
1 tablespoon of salt.

DIRECTIONS—First, get the beef for the soup from the lower part of the round; cut it in small pieces and put to boil in cold water; let boil for about five hours, then strain and put away to cool; if any fat raises, skim off; return to the kettle and add the onion and celery, chopped; boil half an hour and strain again and serve while hot. Some like a little of each sage, thyme and parsley, but is quite nice withont.

TOMATO SOUP.

1 pint of beef stock,
1 can of tomatoes,
2 tablespoons of butter,
1 tablespoon of flour,
2 onions,
¼ teaspoon of pepper, 1 teaspoon of salt,
2 tablespoons of sauce.

DIRECTIONS—Put into a frying pan some butter, and when hot put the onions, chopped, and tomatoes after they have been drained; cook for more than a half hour, remove from stove, press through a sieve and return to the fire, adding the beef stock; stir the flour in after dissolving it in a little warm water; then add the pepper, salt and sauce. Serve hot. Use any kind of sauce that is liked.

A THICKENING FOR SOUPS.

May be made by stirring a tablespoon of butter with one tablespoon of flour; melt the butter in a frying pan and add the flour; stir until it is a nice brown, and a small quantity added to soups make them them a dark color when it is desired.

BOUILLON.

2½ lbs. of lean beef,
½ gallon of cold water,
1 onion,
1 tablespoon of salt,
1 head of celery,
1 teaspoon of pepper,
1 egg,

DIRECTIONS—Chop the beef fine, put in a kettle, add the cold water, salt, pepper and onion chopped fine, and the head of celery; boil over a moderate fire for two hours, then set where it will boil brisk, then skim; set over a moderate fire again and boil for four hours; strain and return to the kettle; beat the white of the egg and add also the shell of the egg; let boil ten minutes, put in a cup of cold water, remove from the fire and strain. Serve in bouillon cups.

COCOANUT SOUP.

½ lb of cocoanut,
3 pints of beef broth,
1 cup of rice,
1 teaspoon of salt,
¼ teaspoon of mace,
1 cup of good cream,

DIRECTIONS—Grate cocoanut, add to the beef broth, cook about an hour slowly; strain the liquor and add the cup of rice, after it has been ground; season with the salt and mace; add a little cayenne pepper if desired; and just before sending to the table, add the cream after being well heated.

LOBSTER SOUP.

Use chicken stock or broth for the foundation; pick a can of lobsters to pieces; add two quarts of the broth; one onion chopped fine and a stalk of celery; cook one hour, then strain and add about a pint more broth; now add one cup of good cream, salt and pepper to taste.

CELERY SOUP

1 pint of chicken broth,
10 stalks of celery,
3 pints of water,
1 teaspoon of flour,
1 onion,
½ teaspoon of mace,
1 pint of new milk,
1 tablespoon of butter,
1½ teaspoons of salt,
1 teaspoon of pepper,
1 egg,
1 cup of whipped cream.

DIRECTIONS—Cut the celery in small pieces; put to cook in the water; cook one-half hour; remove and put in the broth; add the milk and onion chopped, and mace; add the butter with the flour. Before adding cook one-half an hour and strain; whip the egg and also the cup of cream and add just before serving.

OYSTER SOUP

Take the liquor from one can of fresh oysters, add three pints of milk and three tablespoons of butter; put the oysters in after it is well heated; let them remain till they are done sufficiently, then skim them out and salt and pepper the soup and pour over the oysters boiling hot, and serve immediately. Oysters are done sufficiently when the edges begin to ruffle, and should not be cooked any longer after this.

HOW TO ADD EGGS TO SOUPS

Whip the eggs till very light, then add some water to the beaten eggs and add to the soup by degrees, stirring all the time to prevent it from being in lumps.

CHICKEN SOUP.

Dress and joint a young chicken and put to cook in three quarts of cold water; salt to taste and cook till very tender or till the bones fall out, then remove the chicken and reserve to make chicken croquettes, and season with butter with a tablespoon of flour dredged in; just before serving add a small bunch of celery; serve while very hot; strain before serving.

CHICKEN SOUP WITH CORN.

Add to one quart of chicken broth one large cup of green corn, which has been chopped fine; add a cup of cream, and salt and pepper. If cream is used no butter need be added, if milk, add butter the size of a walnut. Let boil one-half an hour and strain and serve while very hot.

TO MAKE NOODLE SOUP.

Take a medium sized soup bone; put on to cook with one gallon of cold water; salt and let it boil until it begins to get tender; add any kind of vegetable liked; add pepper and the noodles which can be prepared as follows: Two eggs, one teaspoon of salt, one fourth of a cup of water; the water must be cold; make the dough very stiff, roll thin and put around a stick about two inches thick; put in a warm place to dry and when needed to use break off as much as needed, and add to your soup; they cook very easily; twenty minutes is all that is necessary for them to cook.

A GOOD BEEF SOUP.

Take a three pound soup-bone, put to cook in four quarts of cold water; add salt, and cook two hours; then add one large onion, two potatoes, one turnip and a sprig of parsley; chop all these together before adding to the soup; boil until the vegetables are tender, then break three eggs in your soup tureen after having them whisked light; strain the soup in by degrees, as this will prevent the eggs from curdling, and will cook them sufficiently. too; this makes a very nice beef soup and is easily made.

CURRY SOUP.

2 quarts of veal broth,
2 medium-size onions,
1 bunch of parsley,
1 chicken,
1 tablespoon of curry powder,
1 lemon,
1 cup of cream,

DIRECTIONS—Put the veal broth in a kettle; add the onion chopped fine and parsley shredded; let it boil and simmer fifteen minutes, then strain; have the chicken jointed and add this to the broth, with the curry powder; let all this boil gently till the chicken is very tender. Just before serving add the juice of the lemon and one cup of boiled cream.

TO MAKE CURRY POWDER FOR SOUPS.

½ ounce of pepper,
2   "   " tumeric,
2   "   " coriander seed,
¼   "   " cayenne pepper,
½   "   " cardamoms,
½   "   " cinnamon,
¼   "   " cumin seed,

DIRECTIONS—Mix all the ingredients together; powder them or have it done at druggist's, as most of them cannot be procured else where. This powder is fine to put in gravies and soups, but very little is necessary.

SAUCES AND GRAVIES.

CREAM SAUCE.

2 eggs,
⅔ cup of white sugar,
1 glass of brandy,
1 teaspoon of flavoring,
1 cup of cream.

DIRECTIONS—Use the whites of the eggs, beaten stiff; then add sugar and brandy; alternate until all is used; add the cream hot; for flavoring use vanilla, orange or any kind that is preferred. Beat well and serve at once.

MAYONAISE.

1 teaspoon of mustard,
4 tablespoons of butter,
1 teaspoon of sugar,
½ teaspoon of salt,
3 eggs,
½ cup of sweet cream,
½ cup of vinegar.

DIRECTIONS—Put the mustard in a pan, add the melted butter next, then sugar and salt; break in the eggs beat well; add cream and the vinegar, a little at a time; mix well; place the pan in hot water; stir until thick.

TO MAKE DRAWN BUTTER SAUCE.

One-half pint of hot water; one-fourth teaspoon of salt; one tablespoon of flour. one-fourth cup of butter. Cream the butter and flour together, then add the water, a little at a time, keeping it very hot; stir all the time till the sauce comes to a boiling point. After removing from the stove add salt to taste. Some like a little lemon juice added, but if properly made it is quite nice without.

CREAMY SAUCE.

1 tablespoon of butter,
3 tablespoons of sugar,
½ cup of cream,
½ teaspoon of vanilla.

DIRECTIONS—Cream the butter, add the sugar gradually, beating all the time; when very light add the milk, a little at a time. Just before serving stand the bowl containing the sauce in a pan of hot water for a few seconds, beating hard. It should be light and frothy.

MUSHROOM SAUCE.

1 can of mushroom,
2 tablespoons of wine,
1 lemon,
1 tablespoon of sauce,
2 cups of water,
2 tablespoons of flour.

DIRECTIONS—Mix butter and flour together after slightly melting the butter; add the water, lemon juice and sauce; use any good sauce that is preferred; add the mushroom sliced; add the wine last, using sherry if it can be procured.

A GOOD HARD SAUCE.

½ cup of butter,
1 cup of sugar,
1 lemon.

DIRECTIONS—Melt the butter slightly, then add sugar and cream; mix well together; add the lemon juice and a part of the rind grated; put in a deep dish and smooth over with a knife and set away in a cool place. To be eaten with plum puddings.

CRANBERRY SAUCE.

Cook berries very tender. For a quart of berries allow two cups of sugar and one pint of water; when done remove and let cool. Serve with meats of any kind.

TOMATO SAUCE FOR MEATS.

1 peck of ripe tomatoes,
½ gallon of cider vinegar,
½ tablespoon of cayenne,
1 teacup of white sugar,
1 teaspoon of salt,
1 teaspoon of spice.

DIRECTIONS—Put the tomatoes in a steamer; let steam until the skins can easily be removed; then put in a pan to cool; remove the skins; mash and press through a colander and season with the spices and pepper; add the sugar, salt and vinegar; put in a porcelain or granite kettle and cook one hour. Bottle and cork and keep in a cool place.

BRANDY SAUCE.

½ cup of water,
¼ cup of brandy,
1 tablespoon of corn starch,
2 small cups of white sugar,
½ cup of butter,
1 teaspoon of vanilla.

DIRECTIONS—Put brandy and water together and let come to a boil; dissolve the corn starch in cold water and add; boil one minute and pour over the sugar and butter, after they have been creamed together; next whip with the egg until very light; flavor with vanilla and it is ready to serve. This is splendid sauce.

TARTARE SAUCE.

¼ cup of good vinegar,
1 tablespoon of capers,
3 cucumber pickles,
1 onion,
¼ cup of mayonnaise.

DIRECTIONS—Chop the pickles fine, also the onions; add the vinegar and mayonnaise; mix it and it is ready to serve. Just before sending to the table add the capers.

CELERY SAUCE.

3 heads of celery,
2 teaspoons of flour,
2 tablespoons of butter,
½ teaspoon of salt,
¼ teaspoon of pepper,
1½ cups of sweet cream.

DIRECTIONS—Chop and stew the celery in just enough water to cover it; then cream the butter and flour together; add salt and pepper; then add this to the celery, also the cream; stew a minute and serve. Excellent with poultry.

LEMON SAUCE.

1 lemon,
1 large cup of sugar,
½ cup of water,
1 tablespoon of flour,
¼ cup of butter.

DIRECTIONS—Slice the lemon after removing the seeds and outside rind; add the water; sift the flour and sugar together; add butter; set on to boil and cook till it thickens. This sauce is excellent with lemon pudding.

WHIPPED CREAM SAUCE.

1½ cups of good sweet cream,
4 eggs,
½ cup of white sugar,
1 teaspoon of vanilla.

DIRECTIONS—Have the cream very cold and whip stiff; beat the whites of the eggs; add the sugar and flavoring; mix well with the cream. Serve with any kind of pudding.

ASPARAGUS SAUCE.

1 quart of asparagus heads,
1 quart of hot water,
1½ cups of sweet cream,
1 tablespoon of butter,
½ teaspoon of salt,
¼ teaspoon of pepper.

DIRECTIONS—Wash the asparagus and let stand a few minutes in cold water; then put on to cook in the hot water with the salt in it; cook till done; then drain off the water; add the cream, butter and pepper; shake up well and serve.

WHITE SAUCE FOR FISH.

2 tablespoons of flour,
2 tablespoons of butter,
½ teacup of fish liquor,
3 tablespoons of cream,
1 teaspoon of parsley.

DIRECTIONS—Cream butter and flour together; add the liquor in which the fish were boiled; add the milk; boil a few minutes and stir in the chopped parsley. This is very nice with the addition of a little celery salt. If not quite salt enough from the butter, add a pinch of salt.

STRAWBERRY SAUCE.

¼ cup of butter,
1 pint of ripe strawberries,
1 egg.

DIRECTIONS—Beat the butter and sugar to a cream; wash the berries and drain them; add the sugar and butter to the strawberries, and beaten white of the egg; beat up well; serve with bread and butter; this sauce will be found very nice and rich.

A COLD PUDDING SAUCE.

2 small cups of sugar,
¾ cup of good butter,
1 egg,
1 lemon.

DIRECTIONS—Beat the butter to a cream; add the sugar and lemon juice; whip the whites of the egg stiff, and add; heap the sauce roughly, on a dish; set on ice till ready to serve.

OYSTER SAUCE.

½ can of fresh oysters,
¼ cup of sweet cream,
⅓ cup of butter,
½ teaspoon of pepper,
1 teaspoon of salt.

DIRECTIONS—Chop the oysters fine; add the butter, melted, cream, pepper and salt; mix and set on back part of the stove, boil for a minute, and serve with baked fish.

BLACK GRAVY, NO. 1.

Take the grease after cooking ham, let it get very hot, and put the flour in and let it cook thoroughly, before adding any water; then add the water cold; boil till well done, and pour around the ham, or in a gravy tureen; powdered sage added to gravy made from chicken or meat makes a very nice addition; to be served with any kind of poultry or meat.

ANOTHER METHOD OF MAKING BLACK GRAVY.

Brown the flour in a pan in the oven and proceed as in No. 1, only use the browned flour; this makes a somewhat darker gravy but is not relished as much as the other by most people; as in browning the flour it is so apt to scorch unless great care is taken; it is a good plan to keep a tin can and have a supply on hand, so when needed it will be ready prepared.

SALADS.

CHICKEN SALAD.

2 breasts of chickens,
2 heads of celery,
2 eggs,
4 tablespoons of butter,
1 teaspoon of pepper,
2 tablespoons of salt,
½ teaspoon of mustard,
1 cup of vinegar.

DIRECTIONS—Cook the chicken tender, cut in thin slices; prepare the celery in the same way; mix the other ingredients together, and cook; then cool, before pouring over the the salad; in adding the butter and vinegar, melt the butter and add it alternately, a little at a time or the vinegar will cause the egg to curdle.

SWEET BREAD SALAD.

After washing the sweet breads well, let them remain in ice water or water that is very cold, for an hour; remove to a kettle with enough water to cover; then having it salted, boil till tender; they will cook in less than an hour; remove again to a pan of very cold water, let remain for a few minutes, five minutes will be sufficient; now proceed to mix by allowing one cup of chopped celery to one cup of minced sweet breads; serve with cream mayonaise; garnish with lettuce leaves.

EGG SALAD, NO. 1.

6 hard boiled eggs,
2 tablespoons of sugar,
1 teaspoon of salt,
½ teaspoon of mustard,
2 tablespoons of butter,
½ cup of vinegar,
1 cup of sweet cream,
¼ teaspoon of black pepper.

DIRECTIONS—Boil the eggs hard; slice thin, and make the dressing; add the sugar, salt, pepper and mustard, together; melt the butter, and add the vinegar and butter alternately; and last the cream by degrees; place the sliced eggs in a salad dish; pour over the dressing; garnish with thin slices of lemon.

SALMON SALAD, NO. 2.

1 lb can of salmon,
1 head of celery,
¼ teaspoon of pepper,
2 tablespoons of salad oil,
4 tablespoons of vinegar,
2 teaspoons of salt.

DIRECTIONS—Chop the salmon, also the celery; reserve the leaves of the celery, to garnish with; after the meat and celery are mixed, put in a salad bowl, and garnish with the leaves; mix the dressing made by adding the oil, vinegar, salt and pepper; pour over the salmon, and serve at once.

EGG SALAD, NO. 2.

6 heads of lettuce,
5 eggs.

DIRECTIONS—Boil the eggs hard; clean the lettuce, put in a salad bowl; slice the eggs over the lettuce and pour over the following dressing, and serve;

DRESSING FOR EGG SALAD—
1 cup of sour cream,
1 tablespoon of sugar,
2 tablespoons of lemon juice,
1 teaspoon of salt,
¼ teaspoon of cayenne pepper,
2 tablespoons of vinegar.

DIRECTIONS—Put salt, pepper and sugar together; add lemon juice, and vinegar; last, the cream after beating well with a fork; set on ice; and just before sending to the table pour over the eggs and lettuce; this is also good for any kind of vegetable salad dressing.

LOBSTER SALAD.

To a three pound lobster; take one egg, beat till light; then take the yolks of two hard boiled eggs, beat well together, and drop olive oil a little at a time; keep stirring all the time; then add one teaspoon of ground mustard; salt and pepper to taste; beat until light; then add two tablespoons of good vinegar; cut the lobster in small pieces after boiling tender, and pour over the dressing; and just before serving garnish with the whites of the eggs cut in thin slices and celery leaves.

SALMON SALAD.

1 can of salmon,
1 onion,
1 tablespoon of sugar,
1 teaspoon of salt,
¼ teaspoon of pepper,
4 tablespoons of vinegar,
1 tablespoon of salad oil,
½ teaspoon of mustard,
1 lemon.

DIRECTIONS—Chop the salmon fine, and then proceed to make the dressing; mix the salt, pepper and mustard, sugar after these are well mixed; chop the onion fine; add the juice of the lemon and oil; stand five minutes, then pour over the chopped salmon and mix lightly; this is a very nice salad.

CUCUMBER SALAD.

3 cucumbers,
1 teaspoon of salt,
½ teaspoon of pepper,
½ teaspoon of celery salt,
½ cup of good vinegar,
1 tablespoon of oil.

DIRECTIONS—Cut off about an inch from each end of the cucumber, as that imparts the bitter flavor; slice about one-fourth of an inch thick; sprinkle the salt and pepper over them, and set on ice until thoroughly chilled; remove and add the vinegar and oil alternately; now you have a nice, crisp salad.

OYSTER SALAD.

1½ pints of oysters,
2 heads of celery,
1 tablespoon of oil,
1 teaspoon of salt,
3 tablespoons of vinegar,
2 tablespoons of lemon juice,
½ teaspoon of pepper,
¼ cup of mayonaise.

DIRECTIONS—Put oysters in pan and cook slightly, do not add any water, the liquor of the oysters being sufficient. When they begin to boil turn into a colander; when drained place in a dish, and add the oil; use any good salad oil; now add salt, pepper and lemon juice; set on ice until very cold; chop the celery very fine; put in a dish with a lump of ice; when ready to serve, drain the water off, mix with the oysters; put all into a salad bowl, and pour over the mayonaise; garnish with some of the celery leaves, and serve at once. Use any recipe desired for the mayonaise; several will be found in this book.

CABBAGE SALAD.

¼ of a cabbage head,
4 eggs,
½ cup of sugar,
1 teaspoon of salt,
½ teaspoon of black pepper,
2 tablespoons of butter,
1 teaspoon of mustard,
1 cup of vinegar.

DIRECTIONS—Wash and slice cabbage fine; remove any tough or wilted leaves; boil eggs hard, slice them in rings, mix lightly together; then add the mustard, salt and pepper and also the sugar; drop the melted butter alternately with the vinegar; toss lightly and arrange in a dish, and garnish with celery leaves.

A GOOD SALAD.

3 tablespoons of cheese,
½ teaspoon of salt,
2 tablespoons of vinegar,
¼ teaspoon of black pepper,
2 tablespoons of butter.

DIRECTIONS—Grate the cheese fine; add vinegar by degrees, then salt, pepper and melted butter; beat until well mixed; and serve garnished with lettuce leaves.

A GOOD POTATO SALAD.

6 medium sized potatoes,
2 small onions,
2 small beets,
2 tablespoons of butter,
1 teacup of vinegar,
1 teaspoon of mustard.

DIRECTIONS—Boil the potatoes in their jackets, slice rather thick; chop the onions fine and add; cook beets until tender and chop them; add the melted butter and vinegar a little at a time; and sprinkle with salt and pepper; put in a dish, garnish with the beets and parsley, add mustard seed last.

CABBAGE SALAD NO. 2.

1 tablespoon of sugar,
1 medium sized cabbage,
1 cup of cream dressing,
1 pint of whipped cream,
½ cup of vinegar,
1 teaspoon of mustard seed.

DIRECTIONS—Shave the cabbage, put in cold water, let stand a few minutes; drain, and sprinkle pepper and salt and mustard seed; add cream dressing; mix lightly; put in a dish and serve garnished with thin slices of eggs.

LETTUCE SALAD. NO. 2.

3 heads of nice lettuce,
½ cup of vinegar,
¼ teaspoon of pepper,
½ teaspoon of mustard,
1 tablespoon of salad oil,
3 hard boiled eggs,
1 teaspoon of sugar,
1 teaspoon of salt.

DIRECTIONS—Boil the eggs and rub the yolks to a powder; slice the white in rings; put the mustard, pepper, salt and sugar together, add the powdered yolks; then add the oil and vinegar alternately; beat up lightly with two forks; put the lettuce in a dish and pour over the dressing, and the slices of the eggs around as a garnish.

TONGUE SALAD.

1 beef tongue,
1 tablespoon of salt,
4 good sized potatoes,
1 head of celery.
3 hard boiled eggs,
2 tablespoons of butter,
1 teaspoon of mustard,
⅓ teaspoon of pepper,
4 tablespoons of vinegar,
1 cup of liquid.

DIRECTIONS—Cook tongue very tender and slice thin; boil eggs hard and slice the whites in rings; cook potatoes and slice thin; use the liquor the tongue was boiled in: add mustard, salt and pepper and mix lightly; chop and add celery. This is a splendid salad.

CHICKEN SALAD—EXCELLENT.

1 chicken,
½ cup of vinegar,
¼ cup of butter,
½ teaspoon of celery seed,
¼ teaspoon of pepper,
1 cup of sweet cream,
5 medium sized potatoes.

DIRECTIONS—Boil the chicken very tender, remove from the bone, chop very fine, put into a mixing bowl; add the butter after it has been melted, and vinegar, alternate a little at a time; then chop potatoes, after they have been boiled tender; add to this the celery seed, pepper and salt; the cream last; mix well; set away awhile before serving; if made exactly by this recipe, will be found as nice as any chicken salad can be made. Some like it garnished with thin slices of lemon.

Eggs and Omelettes.

BOILED EGGS.

Choose fresh eggs to boil; if doubtful about their being fresh drop in cold water, if not good they will rise to the top of the water; have the water at a boiling point, put in with a spoon or skimmer, and let remain in the water for three minutes, if wished to be rather soft, or if wanted hard boiled let them remain five or more minutes; skim out on a hot dish, and serve at once.

CURRIED EGGS.

½ pint of beef broth,
8 eggs,
1 large onion,
½ tablespoon curry powder,
1 cup of cream.

DIRECTIONS—Slice onion and fry brown in some butter; heat the cream and thicken a little with flour or rice powder; have the eggs boiled, and sliced; add to the broth; then cream, curry powder and onions; pour over the sliced eggs, mix well, and serve while hot.

POACHED EGGS.

Use fresh eggs—eggs that are poached if not fresh are more easily detected than in any other way; break the eggs on a flat dish; have the water boiling hot, put one egg in at a time till all are in; cook briskly, cover over for a few minutes till the yolks are covered with the whites of the eggs; skim out with a skimmer; put on a platter; add some small pieces of butter, pepper and salt; then cover over for a few minutes and send to the table.

VEGETABLE OMELET.

Take cucumbers, potatoes, onions, green peas, tomatoes, and mushrooms; chop them fine after being cooked tender; add some pepper and salt and cream enough to make it the consistency wanted; put on the stove and heat till hot, but do not let it boil; have your omelet ready; put in the pan and when ready to roll together add this mixture; these are very nice; the onions may be omitted if disliked.

TO STUFF EGGS.

Use any number of eggs; boil till hard; put in cold water to remove the shells; cut in halves, take out the yolks and rub them to a powder; add some finely minced ham and salt and pepper, and some powdered crackers, and as much melted butter as will make it a little soft; set whites on a platter, fill in with the mixture; put in a pan, set in the oven a few minutes and serve with celery.

TOMATO OMELET.

Slice very ripe tomatoes, fry in butter after draining them, as well as you can; make the omelet and cook as usual, and put some of the slices of the tomatoes between.

FRIED EGGS.

The better way to fry eggs, for any one that objects to them being too greasy, is to use a very little meat fryings—ham is the best; put into gem pans, set them on the stove till hot; put one egg in each place or cup, and set in the oven a few minutes, until sufficiently cooked, and they are ready to serve.

CAULIFLOWER OMELET.

1 pint of cauliflower,
5 eggs,
1 large cup of milk,
¼ teaspoon of pepper,
1 teaspoon of salt.

DIRECTIONS—Chop the cauliflower fine, after being cooked till very tender; add the beaten yolks, then the cauliflower and whites of the eggs, whisked light; last, pepper and salt; butter a frying pan and turn the omelet in, after it is hot; cook a few minutes, turn one-half over the other, and serve while hot.

MEAT OMELETS.

Make an omelet by any of the recipes found in this book, and chop very fine any cold meat, chicken or beef; season to suit taste, and before folding over your omelet, place some of this between the omelet and it is ready to serve; this is a very nice way to use cold meats.

A PLAIN OMELET.

For several in family, use about nine eggs, beat them separately; add to the yolks two cups of sweet milk, some pepper and salt; do not beat the yolks to much; whip the whites stiff; add them and mix well together; put some butter in a pan and put your omelet in; cook quickly, but be careful not to brown it; serve while hot.

FRENCH OMELET.

1 cup of sweet milk,
1 cup of bread crumbs,
¼ teaspoon of pepper,
1 small teaspoon of salt,
6 eggs.

DIRECTIONS—Beat the eggs separately; heat the milk to a boiling point, then pour over the bread crumbs; add the yolks of the eggs, salt and pepper, last the whites beaten still; put on a frying pan with some butter, put the mixture in and cook three minutes fold over, and it is ready to serve.

BAKED EGGS.

Break as many eggs as are needed for the meal, into a plate; grease a baking dish; put in the eggs, sprinkle slightly with salt and pepper; put in a small piece of butter on top of each, bake well or rare done, as preferred; take up on small egg plates, and serve with a sprig of parsley on each egg.

BREADED EGGS.

Pour hot water over any number of eggs wished to be served, let simmer, but not boil, a few minutes, not over five; pour this water off and put cold water on so the shells will be easily removed; when cold remove the shells and slice one egg in three pieces lengthwise, dip in melted butter then in bread crumbs, after dipping in beaten egg, fry in hot lard or butter. These are nice for lunches, or if used while warm are nice with cream sauce.

TO BAKE AN OMELET.

Place a pan on top of stove; grease it slightly; have the omelet ready, put in, and place in the oven; let brown slightly; pour on a hot platter and serve.

SCRAMBLED EGGS.

Use any number of eggs desired; allow one tablespoon of cream to each egg; also a pinch of salt and pepper; beat the eggs well, season, turn into a pan, stir until done; serve very hot with toast, or any kind of meats.

CHEESE OMELET.

¼ teaspoon of salt,
4 eggs,
1 pinch of pepper,
¼ cup of milk,
2 tablespoons of cheese.

DIRECTIONS—Beat the eggs separately; add the milk to the yolks, salt and pepper, then the beaten whites of the eggs; last, the grated cheese; put in a hot frying pan; cook till it sets, and turn over, and serve while very hot.

EGG SPONGE.

½ dozen eggs,
1 teaspoon of salt,
¼ teaspoon of pepper,
1 tablespoon of butter.

DIRECTIONS—Separate the yolks from the whites; whip the whites separately, till very light; put a spoonful in an egg cup, make a small place in the center, put a yolk in, and so on till all is used; sprinkle with salt and pepper; set the cups in a pan in boiling water, send to the oven for about two minutes; serve at once with a very small piece of butter on each one; serve in the cups.

EGGS WITH FRIED HAM.

Slice the ham thin; have a pan hot, put the ham in, let brown nicely on both sides; put on a buttered platter; keep where it will be warm, break in some eggs, fry them and put around the ham on the platter; serve at once.

OMELET NO 2.

Take five eggs, one pint of new milk, butter the size of an egg, and one tablespoon of flour; whip the yolks and whites of the eggs separately; melt the butter and add to the yolks; next add the flour, milk, and salt enough to suit taste; add the beaten whites last; put in a frying pan, and when done sufficiently turn over and let remain about a minute. Serve at once.

CREAM EGGS ON TOAST.

Toast some stale light bread; put to one-half dozen slices of bread, one cup of sweet cream; heat it slightly, and dip with a spoon over the slices of bread; have some eggs broken on a plate; put some cream in a pan; pour the eggs in and cook as qnick as possible; salt and pepper; put a spoonful over each piece of bread; send to the table immediately.

EGGS FOR LUNCH.

Boil the eggs till very hard; when cold cut them lengthwise; rub the yolks and some cold chicken chopped; add cream, some celery and grated cheese; after all this is chopped fine and mixed well, fill in the halves and put together and wrap in tissue paper. If liked, can after being put together, dip in beaten egg and rolled in crackers and fried in hot lard, but is quite nice without.

FRIZZLED MEAT WITH EGGS.

½ pound of shaved ham,
3 eggs,
1 cup of hot water,
1 tablespoon of butter.

DIRECTIONS.—After shaving the ham, or dried beef, if preferred to the ham, put to soak in the cup of hot water and soak for fifteen minutes, keeping it hot; then beat the eggs well; put the butter in a frying pan and when it gets very hot add the meat and stir till the slices begin to curl up; then set the pan over hot water; add the eggs and stir till they are cooked; it will be hot enough over the water to cook them sufficient. Serve while hot.

MACARONI WITH EGGS.

After boiling the macaroni till tender, put one cup of milk in a pan, and add three eggs, beaten light; use the whole eggs; season with salt and pepper; put the macaroni in a pan and pour this over; put in the oven for a few minutes, and it is ready to serve.

HAM AND POACHED EGGS.

Slice the ham thin; fry a nice brown; put on in a pan in some hot water salted; have the pan slightly greased before putting the water in; break the eggs in; have water enough to cover them; when done sufficient remove to the plate of ham, putting an egg on each piece of ham, and a small piece of butter and some pepper on top of each egg, and they are ready for the table.

ESCALLOPED EGGS.

5 eggs,
½ teaspoon of pepper,
1 teaspoon of salt,
1 tablespoon butter.

DIRECTIONS.—Beat the eggs separately; put the beaten whites in a baking dish; make a hollow in the center; beat the yolks, and add the pepper and salt; sprinkle a little cracker dust over them; add the butter; pour this in the whites and bake five minutes and serve very hot.

HOW TO PRESERVE EGGS, NO. 1.

Select what you know to be fresh eggs; take a stone jar the size you wish to hold the number of eggs you desire to keep; put a layer of salt, then one of eggs; be sure and have the small end of the eggs down; next a layer of salt and eggs, till the jar is full; have a very thick layer of salt at the top. This will be found an excellent way to keep eggs.

HOW TO PRESERVE EGGS, NO. 2.

This recipe is some more trouble than No 1. Three teacups of salt; to this add a piece of lime about the size of a teacup; put this into a jar and slack with three quarts of hot water; let stand till perfectly cold; pour off and add the salt; stir till it dissolves; then pour over the eggs. A large stone jar is best. Have enough of the water to cover them.

SANDWICHES.

TO MAKE SANDWICHES.

A nice sandwich requires no little pains to have them what they should be. In the first place, the bread that is used should be nice and fresh, the ham cooked very tender, but not so much that it will not slice nicely; cut ham and bread in thin slices; first, remove the crust and butter nicely; put a liberal piece of ham between the slices of bread. If wanted for any occasion in which everything is wished to be as dainty as possible, tie each one with tiny ribbon and have a nice little bow; will look very nice.

EGG SANDWICHES.

Use good light bread or buns; butter them; have the eggs boiled hard; slice the egg round ways; put on one slice; then put chopped celery, pickles chopped, or if salad is preferred, use that; put the other piece of bread over and cut in nice squares; if the piece of bread is large it will made two sandwiches.

A FINE DRESSING FOR SANDWICHES.

½ ℔ butter,
1 cup of vinegar,
2 tablespoons of mustard,
3 tablespoons of salad oil,
1 pinch of cayenne pepper,
1 pinch of salt,
1 egg.

DIRECTIONS—Cream the butter; add the mustard, pepper, salt and salad oil; now add the vinegar and beat up well; last add the yolk of the egg; mix all well together; spread on the slices of bread, and put the chopped ham on. This makes a very rich dressing for sandwiches, if properly made.

FISH SANDWICHES.

Take bits of white fish, or any fish that has been left over from a meal, chop fine; take eggs, two is sufficient for two cupsful of chopped fish; beat the eggs well, add oil till they begin to thicken; stir the fish in; add some vinegar, just enough to taste, and salt and pepper; cut thin slices of bread, spread with this and cut in squares, and serve.

MIXED SANDWICHES—FINE.

Chop equal parts of chicken, tongue and ham; after chopping these together, divide, and put with one part, two tablespoons of melted butter, one tablespoon of salad oil, one tablespoon of prepared mustard, the powdered yolks of three hard boiled eggs, some pepper and salt; butter some thin slices of bread and put the meat between, and serve.

LOBSTER SANDWICHES.

Put into a pan one tablespoon of butter and let it get warm; add one-half cup of hot water; add a teaspoon of flour, (it might be added to the butter before the water is added); now have the lobster meat chopped fine and add enough to make it about as thick as hash; cut thin slices of bread; butter them; put in the oven till slightly browned; then put some of the mixture between the slices.

CUCUMBER SANDWICHES.

Cut thin slices of bread and butter them; have the cucumbers sliced thin; and some good mayonaise; spread the bread with mayonaise; then put the cucumber slices on; butter the other slice for the top, and put in a cool place till ready to serve. These are very nice for one that likes cucumbers. The colder they are kept the better they are.

OYSTER SANDWICHES.

1 dozen fresh oysters,
1 tablespoon of butter,
1 teaspoon of salt,
½ teaspoon of pepper,
1 cup of cracker crumbs,
1 egg,
1 teaspoon of lemon juice.

DIRECTIONS—Chop the oysters; add the butter, salt and pepper, and put them to cook in their own liquor, cook five minutes, and add the cracker crumbs and the egg, after beating it up well; stir till it thickens; then add the lemon juice and pour out on a plate; when cold cut in clices and it is ready to put between the bread.

VEGETABLES.

TO BOIL VEGETABLES.

To boil vegetables, it is always better to cook them in soft water. If soft water can not be obtained, put in a small amount of baking soda in the water before putting on to cook. Wash all vegetables thoroughly before putting on to cook, and water that is used for cooking should be fresh, as allowing it to stand renders it unfit for cooking purposes; they should be cooked very fast, as any vegetable that is green retains its color better than when cooked slow. Vegetables gathered fresh are better, but if obliged to use them a little stale, lay in cold water some time before cooking; this will freshen them some. Vegetables that are raised by an artificial means are not healthy, or vegetables used too green. In cooking vegetables that have a bad odor, drop a piece of bread crust in while boiling, or some red pepper will answer the purpose. Add sugar to peas, beets, squash, corn, turnips and pumpkins.

FRIED POTATOES.

Peel your potatoes and wash them; cut in thick slices and then cut the slices in squares; have the grease very hot; put them in and fry until a nice brown; skim them out in a colander. They are very pretty prepared this way.

DRY LIMA BEANS.

Soak the beans over night; in the morning change the water, and when time to put on to cook, put them on in fresh water; have the water hot and salted a little; it requires about two hours to cook; when done, season with butter and a spoonful of flour added; next add a cup of cream, and put in with the beans; cook a few minutes and serve. For this amount it will take about one quart of beans, after they are soaked.

POTATO CROQUETTES.

Take mashed potatoes; mix some butter and beaten whites of eggs in them; then salt and pepper; mix well, make out with the hands into cone shapes; dip in the yolks of the eggs, then in crackers and fry in hot lard a golden brown.

PRINCESS POTATOES.

Use cold, boiled potatoes; slice lengthwise, in thick slices; dip in egg, then fry in hot grease till brown; serve while hot.

POTATOES BAKED WITH BEEF.

Wash and pare the potatoes; they must not be too large; put them in the pan with the beef, dip the gravy over them, until they are done; it will take about one hour to cook well done.

BAKED SWEET POTATOES.

Wash medium sized potatoes; put in a baking pan and bake in a quick oven; they ought to be served at once.

BAKED SWEET PUMPKIN.

Cut the pumpkin in slices; put in a baking pan, with the rind next to the pan; be careful to remove all the seeds and scrape a little below the seeds; put lumps of butter over each piece, and bake in a very hot oven; serve in the rind, or may be scooped out in a dish; serve while very hot.

BROWNED TURNIPS.

Cook the turnips till almost done; skim out and dip in butter, and fry in hot grease, brown on both sides. Are nice to serve with any kind of game.

BOILED TURNIPS.

Select medium sized turnips; peel and slice them; put on to cook in salted water; when done, pour all the water off that remains; season with butter and some pepper, sprinkled on.

BOILED ONIONS.

Use medium sized onions and of uniform size; peel and put them in a stew pan and cover with hot water; cook about twenty minutes; then pour the water off, as onions have a better flavor to have the water changed; put hot water over them again, and salt it a little; when done pour the water off again and pour over them, a cup of cream and some melted butter; dish up after it stands a few minutes; pepper them and send to the table.

MASHED SWEET POTATOES.

Steam the potatoes; when done peel them and mash; put on a tin and spread with butter, sprinkle some sugar over and set in the oven until they brown; put a knife under the side and slip off onto a plate and serve.

TO COOK SPINACH.

Wash and put in a kettle with enough water to cover; have the water salted slightly; cook till tender; drain and chop fine, and add a cup of milk and a piece of butter; pepper and salt; cook a few minutes; put in a dish and garnish with thin slices of hard boiled eggs.

A NICE WAY TO COOK SWEET POTATOES.

Boil large sweet potatoes; when done pare carefully and arrange in a baking dish; sprinkle with sugar and small piece of butter; put a cup of good cream on the stove and heat it till it almost reaches a boil; set it in the oven for a few minutes and it is ready to serve.

BAKED STUFFED POTATOES.

Use medium sized potatoes; cut the potatoes out inside till only about one-fourth of an inch thick; fill in with minced ham and chopped onions, salt and pepper; fill the potatoes; set in a pan; add some hot water and butter; set in a quick oven and cook till they are well done. They are better if basted often while cooking; when done remove and take some cream and flour and make a gravy and pour over the potatoes on the platter.

A FANCY DISH OF POTATOES.

Cook and mash as usual; put on a tin and make up in a pyramid shape, and take something and make holes over it, about two inches down through the potatoes; have some mashed potato in which there has been some yolk of an egg stirred; take a funnel and fill it with this potato; fill in the holes that have been made in the white potatoes; smooth and butter the top; then set in the oven till brown. This is good, and besides a beautiful dish.

TO COOK SUMMER SQUASH.

Cut in rather thin slices, and dip in egg, then in cracker meal, or dip in butter, and fry in hot grease; they should not be fried too fast, or might not be as tender as liked; some prefer them boiled and mashed, but are usually too watery this way, but when fried are very nice.

BAKED POTATOES.

Choose smooth potatoes to bake, wash them thoroughly, scrape them a little, as they are nicer when done; put in a pan and bake in a quick oven; serve while hot as a baked potato is almost worthless if allowed to get cool.

SUCCOTASH.

Take an equal amount of each lima beans, and corn that has been cut from the cob; put on to cook, and cook about one hour; season with butter and cream, and serve while hot.

DRIED CORN.

Take the amount of corn desired to cook; cover with hot water; soak for five or six hours; drain and put to cook in fresh water; add salt and pepper; cook till tender; season with plenty of butter; cream may be added if liked, but is very good without.

BAKED POTATO ROLLS.

Boil the potatoes in their jackets; peel and mash; make into balls a little larger than a hen egg; dip them in butter, then the beaten yolk of an egg; put on a buttered tin and set in the oven for a few minutes as they brown easily; slip on a platter and send to the table at once.

BAKED POTATOES.

Wash medium sized potatoes and put in a baking pan; set in the oven and bake quick; serve as soon as they are done with plenty of good butter They are nice to break them open just before sending to the table. Sprinkle with salt, pepper; add a good sized piece of butter to each half of potato.

POTATO BALLS.

Take some nice mashed potatoes and make into balls; roll some crackers; beat up an egg; first dip in the egg, then in the crackers; fry in very hot grease.

TO COOK NEW POTATOES.

Wash the potatoes and rub the peel off with a brush; put in to boil in salted water; boil till tender; dip them out in a crock; put it on the back of the stove to keep warm; put some cream and butter in a sauce pan; heat it, and when hot put the potatoes in and shake them up well; put in a covered dish and serve.

YANKEE WAY TO SERVE LETTUCE.

Wash the lettuce; put in a chopping bowl and chop a little; sprinkle some salt and pepper over; while preparing this, have some eggs boiling, and vinegar heating with sugar and meat drippings; after it is well heated, pour over the lettuce in a covered tureen and proceed to get the eggs ready by removing the shells and slicing in rings; garnish the lettuce with them and serve at once.

FRENCH DRESSING FOR LETTUCE.

6 heads of lettuce,
5 teaspoons of salad oil,
2 tablespoons of vinegar,
2 teaspoons salt.

DIRECTIONS.—Pour the oil upon the lettuce, after it has been picked, and put in a salad bowl; then dissolve the salt in the vinegar; pour this slowly on; stir thoroughly, and serve at once.

FRIED CABBAGE.

Slice nice, white cabbage very thin; have some meat drippings in a frying pan; put the cabbage in; salt and pepper, and fry as fast as they can without scorching them; stir often; keep them covered closely when not stirring; when cooked sufficiently serve at once.

MASHED POTATOES.

Cook the potatoes until they are quite tender; pour the water off and let stand for a few minutes in the kettle to steam; then proceed to mash them with a potato masher, the wire ones are the best, as the potatoes are much lighter when thus mashed; beat till they look real white; add some butter and cream, but be careful not to get them too damp, as that will spoil them; always heat the milk or cream that is used in mashed potatoes; do not let it boil; beat up lightly; put in a covered tureen, and serve at once. Potatoes must not stand after being mashed, as they are easily spoiled.

SLAW DRESSING.

2 eggs,
1½ cups of cream,
¼ cup of vinegar,
1 teaspoon of salt,
½ teaspoon of pepper,
½ teaspoon of mustard.

DIRECTIONS.—Chop a small head of cabbage; put in a dish; then beat the eggs well; add cream, next the salt, mustard and pepper; last the vinegar; put in a granite or porcelain kettle; let boil and pour over the cabbage; serve while hot.

BAKED SQUASH.

1 small squash,
½ cup of butter,
1 teaspoon of sugar.

DIRECTIONS.—Slice the squash about three inches wide; arrange the slices in a baking dish—rind down; dust with sugar and the butter cut in pieces; bake till nice and done. Serve in the rind.

STUFFED EGG PLANT.

6 egg plants,
1 cup of chopped ham,
3 tablespoons of bread crumbs,
1 tablespoonful of butter,
1 onion,
½ teaspoon of salt,
¼ teaspoon of pepper.

DIRECTIONS.—Boil egg plant till tender; then prepare the filling by chopping the ham; add bread crumbs, butter, pepper and salt, cut the egg plant in halves; fill each half with a portion of the mixture; bake fifteen minutes.

TO STEW CELERY.

Wash and scrape the celery; cut in small pieces and put to cook in salted water; have the water hot; cook fifteen minutes, and if it is as tender as should be, will be ready to have the the water poured off, and seasoned; season with cream and butter; have a little flour dredged with the butter; cook a few minutes and serve.

ANNAS POTATOES.

Take medium sized potatoes, slice very thin, put in a baking dish, sprinkle over with salt and pepper; then add an onion chopped fine, pour over enough sweet cream and a good sized lump of butter; set in the oven till well done; take out in a dish and garnish with celery tops.

SARATOGA CHIPS.

Pare and slice the potatoes very thin; pour cold water over them and let stand for a few minutes; have some lard toasting hot, cook a few at a time till a nice brown, then dip out into a colander and sprinkle with salt. If a wire basket can be procured it is better to cook them in.

CREAM OF ASPARAGUS.

2 bunches of asparagus,
1 pint of cream,
2 tablespoons of butter,
1 pinch of cayenne,
1 teaspoon of salt,
1 qt. of hot water.

DIRECTIONS:—Boil the asparagus till well done, then pass through a colander; now add one pint of the water that it has been boiled in; add the pepper and salt, scald the cream and add the butter: now put this in the asparagus, stir well and it is ready to serve.

GREEN CORN CROQUETTES.

'Boil the corn on the cob, or if green corn cannot be had, good canned corn will do; remove the corn from the cob; season with salt and pepper; whip some eggs, stir in a little cream, and add a small piece of butter. This cannot be handled with the hands very well, but have some cracker meal ready; dip out by spoonfuls and and drop in the meal, when it can be made out into cone shapes and fried in hot grease, a nice brown.

POTATOES, STEWED.

Pare and slice the potatoes; put in a kettle; cover with hot water; salt, pepper and put in enough butter to make it quite rich; after they are about done, pour off all the water and put in enough milk, in which has been stirred some flour; let cook till it thickens and pour out in a dish and serve.

TO COOK OKRA.

If this is not properly cooked is not at all good; requires careful preparing to be good; first, use only the tender pods; slice them thin; put in boiling water, in which some salt has been added; cook one-half hour; then drain the water off and season with butter, pepper and cream; have the cream and butter heated before putting on; cover for a few minutes and it is ready to serve. Is very nice on toast.

FRIED ONIONS.

Peel and slice them and put in salted water; let come to a boil, pour the water off and add some butter and meat fryings and fry till they are tender and browned slightly. They may be fried in grease alone, and are nice to garnish fried meats with.

CREAMED POTATOES.

Pare and slice medium sized potatoes; put in a sauce pan, pour in enough hot water to cover them; add salt, pepper and butter; cook until well done; remove to a dish; put cream in the pan and heat a few minutes, then pour it over the potatoes and send to the table.

TO COOK KRAUT.

Dip from the barrel or keg what kraut is needed for the meal; if very sour, parboil it by pouring hot water on and let stand a few minutes, then pour this off and add more water; when cooked sufficient, season with fried meat drippings and let cook a few minutes after adding the seasoning. Some prefer kraut boiled like cabbage with meat, but as it has such an odor it is much nicer cooked alone.

TO COOK GREENS.

After picking them look over carefully, and wash in about a dozen pans of water, as they will have more or less sand and dirt in them; when ready to cook, put on in boiling water, salt it a little and cook one hour; season with meat drippings; make them rather greasy; serve with vinegar, mustard and hard boiled eggs. Dandelion, mustard, horse raddish leaves and many other kinds are used.

TO COOK BEETS.

Wash the beets thoroughly, but do not use a knife if you want them to retain their color; cook till tender, but not enough to break the peel; after they are cold, slice into vinegar, unless wished to be used warm, when they are sliced and kept warm, as other vegetables are, and seasoned with butter, pepper and salt.

BAKED TOMATOES.

Choose large, smooth tomatoes; remove the peel, cut out in the centre, leaving only about an inch through to the out side; fill in with bread crumbs, butter, salt, pepper and cream, mixed together; onion may be added if liked; put in a baking pan and bake in a hot oven for twenty minutes; remove and serve at once.

COLD, SLICED TOMATOES.

Take about three good sized tomatoes; choose very ripe ones; slice with a sharp knife, leaving the peel on; put in a glass dish and prinkle with salt and pepper; pour some good cider vinegar over them; let stand a few minutes before serving.

RUTA BAGA.

Cook the same as turnips, but are much harder than turnips, and must be cooked a little longer; season with milk and butter, or may be cooked with pork.

FRIED SALSIFY OR OYSTER PLANT.

Prepare as when boiling cabbage till tender; mash and season, and when cold enough make into cakes and roll in egg, then in cracker crumbs; fry in hot grease till a golden brown.

TO COOK ASPARAGUS.

Take only very tender stalks; chop them and cook in salted water till tender; then drain and add some butter, cream and pepper; shake up and pour in a dish; serve while hot.

HOMINY CROQUETTES.

Take cooked hominy, make into cone shapes; dip in egg, then in cracker meal, then fry in lard until a good brown. These are very nice for breakfast.

FRIED HOMINY.

Use cold hominy that has been boiled; slice and dip in egg and then in meal, and fry in butter until a golden brown; serve at once while hot.

TO STEW TOMATOES.

First select nice tomatoes; scald them enough to remove the peel easily; pare and put them in a kettle in which some butter has been put; chop them up with a spoon, after putting in the kettle; season with salt and pepper; cook briskly for about five minutes, then pour out into a dish and serve.

TO COOK ARTICHOKES.

Scrape and wash them, then put in cold water and let stand awhile, then put on to cook in hot water; cook till quite tender, then remove at once and pour over them some cream sauce.

STEWED SALSIFY.

Wash and scrape the roots well; put them in cold water as they are cleaned; when all are cleaned put to cook, after slicing them in slices; put them in fresh water and cook till tender; pour off the water and add a lump of butter and some cream, in which some flour has been stirred in; let boil again about three minutes; pour in a dish and serve.

GREEN PEAS.

Peas is a vegetable that requires quite a bulk to make the necessary amount required, as they seem to be almost all hull; select nice tender ones: shell them, and put to cook in hot water; salt them; when done, season with butter and cream, or some prefer to omit the cream, and use the butter and pepper to season them; serve while hot.

ONIONS AND TOMATOES FRIED.

Proceed to prepare the onions and tomatoes to fry as they are usually prepared; have the frying pan hot, and some butter and meat fryings put in, and when almost smoking hot, first put the onions in and let them fry about five minutes before putting in the tomatoes; cook till well done; put them in a covered dish and serve.

BAKED EGG PLANT.

Boil till they are very tender; then proceed to mash as potatoes are; season with butter; pepper and salt to taste; butter a baking dish; put a layer of egg plant, then bread crumbs, then the egg plant, till all is used; sprinkle some cracker meal on top, and some small pieces of butter; set in the oven and bake till browned.

FRIED EGG PLANT.

Wash and slice medium sized egg plants, in about four slices; put on in hot water, having it salted a little; boil till they are almost done; skim out; beat up an egg; dip in the egg then in the rolled cracker; fry in butter until well done and they are ready to serve.

BOILED CABBAGE.

To boil cabbage choose a nice head, rather large; quarter it, and have a piece of beef or pork boiling; about one hour before dinner put the cabbage in on top of the meat, as it is much better not to be allowed to lie in the water as it keeps more firm; after it is tender remove and pour some of the meat liquor around in the dish; should be put in a covered dish and not allowed to stand after being taken from the stove; add, while cooking, a small piece of red pepper.

GERMAN WAY TO SERVE LETTUCE.

Take about three heads of nice tender lettuce; pull the heads apart; wash them; cut a good sized slice of ham into small squares; put them in a pan and fry a nice brown; dip the ham out and put in three tablespoons of vinegar; beat two eggs light; add to them, one tablespoon of sugar and one cup of sour cream; mix all together and add to the vinegar; when hot pour over the lettuce and ham, having them in a dish together, first the lettuce, and ham on top.

TO COOK CANNED MUSHROOMS.

Open the can and put them in a kettle; let simmer, but do not let them boil; after they have been on the stove for about five or ten minutes take a sauce pan, put in some butter, salt, pepper and cream; let come to a boil; remove the mushrooms to a covered dish; pour this over them and serve; before putting to cook drain off all the liquor.

TO FRY GREEN TOMATOES.

In preparing green tomatoes to fry, it is some more trouble than the ripe ones. Slice them moderately thin; put in a dish; salt a very little; let stand a few minutes; then drain in a colander; roll them in flour or batter, whichever is desired; fry in hot butter till a crisp brown.

BOILED PARSNIPS.

Scrape and wash parsnips; cut in halves; put them to cook in boiling water; when tender, put in a dish and pour over some melted butter and cream sauce; serve with beef.

TO FRY PARSNIPS.

Boil the parsnips till tender; then cut them in slices; roll in flour and fry in butter till they are brown; put on a hot plate and serve.

STEWED CABBAGE.

Chop the cabbage as for slaw; put into a granite iron kettle; cook till tender; cook very fast, as this is the secret of cabbage retaining their flavor and color; when sufficiently done, season with salt, pepper and butter; cover closely for a few minutes and serve.

ROASTED CORN.

Choose corn not quite as tender as for boiling; clean as usual, use a gridiron; place the ears on it; have bright coals; roast till well done, turning it when done on one side, till all is browned nicely.

CUCUMBERS SERVED WITH CREAM SAUCE.

Slice the cucumbers moderately thick; put to cook in salted water; cook till tender, and pour over them in a dish, some cream sauce. This, when properly cooked, is very nice.

TO FRY CUCUMBERS.

Slice the cucumbers lengthwise; put in salted water for a few minutes; have the water ice cold; dip out and dry on a cloth, or drain in a colander; dredge in flour and fry in hot butter till a nice brown.

TO BOIL GREEN CORN.

Remove the husks and silks from the corn, put in a steamer, set over boiling water, and cook till tender; put in a dish, sprinkle with salt and pepper, pour over some melted butter and keep well covered till ready to serve.

FRIED POTATOES.

Peel any number of potatoes wished; slice lengthwise, moderately thin; have your pan hot and half of each, butter and lard; let it get very hot and put the potatoes in, cover for a few minutes, then remove the lid and cook till they are evenly browned; salt and pepper when first put in.

GREEN BEANS.

String the beans and break in small pieces; put on to cook in hot water, or with meat; if cooked with meat it should be put on about two hours before the beans; when adding the beans put in a little salt, unless the meat is very salty; let cook till done; have a very little water in them when done. If not liked cooked with meat, boil as above in hot water, and season when done with butter and pepper; some add a little cream.

TO COOK DRIED WHITE BEANS.

After washing the beans put them to cook in hot water, in which there has been a piece of meat cooking; the meat should at least be put to cook one hour before adding the beans; cook about two hours more, and if at all tender, they will be sufficiently cooked; some prefer to season any kind of beans with butter; they are very nice either way.

TO SERVE CELERY.

Scrape and wash celery; put in ice water until ready to use; put in glass dish, or regular celery stand; to be served with the vegetables and meats; if dinner is served in courses, celery is removed before the dessert is served.

Puddings and Dumplings.

FIG PUDDING.

2 cups of bread crumbs,
1 large cup of milk,
4 eggs,
½ cup of suet,
½ cup of sugar,
½ dozen figs.

DIRECTIONS:—Soak the bread in the milk; add a pinch of soda; chop the figs and beat the eggs till light; chop the suet and add to the sugar and milk; mix well together; grease a mold and put the pudding in and steam two and a half hours. Serve with any good sauce preferred.

COCOANUT PUDDING.

1 cup of cocoanut,
1 pint of sweet cream,
3 eggs,
½ cup of sugar,
¼ teaspoon of salt.

DIRECTIONS:—Whisk the eggs light; grate the cocoanut and add the cream, sugar and salt; mix together and put in a buttered pan; bake until the custard is set. Good with or without sauce.

BEEF PUDDING.

1 cup of hot water,
2 pounds of good beef,
2 cups of cracker crumbs,
2 eggs,
¼ cup of butter,
2 tablespoons of salt,
1 teaspoon of pepper.

DIRECTIONS—Chop the meat fine; add the crackers, salt, pepper and butter; put the eggs in after beaten up light; add the water; pour in a buttered dish and bake for three quarters of an hour in a moderate oven; turn out on a platter and serve.

PRUNE PUDDING.

4 cups of flour,
1 teaspoon of salt,
½ teaspoon each of cinnamon and nutmeg,
1 cup of suet,
2 cups of prunes,
1 cup of sweet milk,
1 cup of molasses,
1 teaspoon of soda.

DIRECTIONS.—Chop suet fine; rub flour in; add nutmeg and cinnamon; stone the prunes and chop fine; then add the milk, molasses, with the soda dissolved into them; stir well together; pour in buttered molds and steam three hours; serve with foamy sauce.

RICE PUDDING.

1 cup of rice,
1 cup of sugar,
2 cups of milk,
Whites of 2 eggs,
¼ cup of butter,
¼ teaspoon of nutmeg.

DIRECTIONS:—Wash the rice; put in a pudding dish; stir in the sugar and sprinkle nutmeg; chop the butter and put on top; add the milk; bake very slow, that the rice may be well cooked; after it is done, whisk the eggs well, sweeten slightly and flavor with nutmeg, spread on top and return to the oven and brown a little. Serve with whipped cream.

SUET PUDDING.

1 cup of suet,
1 cup of raisins,
¼ teaspoon of cinnamon,
¼ teaspoon of nutmeg,
1 cup of sweet milk,
1 cup of molasses,
1 egg,
1 teaspoon of salt,
3 cups of flour,
1 teaspoon of soda.

DIRECTIONS—Seed the raisins; chop the suet and raisins; add flour, cinnamon and nutmeg; disolve soda in milk, next molasses and salt; beat the egg well; stir well together; put into a buttered pudding dish; boil or steam in a covered dish three hours. Serve with brandy sauce.

STEAMED PUDDING.

1 cup of sugar,
½ cup butter,
3 eggs,—3 cups of flour,
1½ cups of sweet milk,
1 teaspoon of soda,
2 teaspoons of cream of tarter,
1 cup of currants,
1 cup of raisins.

DIRECTIONS:—Cream the butter and sugar together; add the beaten eggs; next, the milk with soda dissolved in it; sift the cream of tartar and flour together, sift into the pudding a little at a time; seed raisins, clean the currants and dry them, dredge in flour and add last; then put into a buttered mold, set over boiling water, steam two hours; serve with cold sauce.

LEMON PUDDING.

¼ lb. of butter,
2 lemons,
6 crackers,
½ cup of good wine,
5 eggs,
1 pint of cream,
1 cup of sugar.

DIRECTIONS:—Cream the butter and sugar together; roll the crackers; add cream, then crackers; extract juice from lemons, put this in, grate the rind of one, then add the wine, and eggs beaten separately; bake with an under crust and pieces of dough on top; served with any sauce preferred.

RICE AND APPLE PUDDING.

½ cup of rice,
1 pint of milk,
2 eggs,
½ cup of jelly,
6 apples,
1 cup of sugar,

DIRECTIONS:—Wash the rice; cook in milk until done; add the yolks and sugar beaten together; boil five minutes longer; cook apples whole after being cored; put in a dish; put the jell in the centre of the apples; put the rice around the apples and beat the whites of the eggs stiff, put over and sprinkle with sugar.

APPLE DUMPLINGS, BAKED—NO 2.

6 large apples,
1 lemon,
½ cup of butter,
1 cup of sugar.

DIRECTIONS:—Make a paste and core the apples by scraping the core out; squeeze the juice from the lemon and roll out the paste and put the apples in; leave a small place at the top; put in some butter and sugar and about a teaspoonful of the lemon juice; put in a baking pan and bake a nice brown. Serve with sauce.

POT PIE DUMPLINGS.

1½ pints of flour,
2 small teaspoons of baking powder,
1 teaspoon of salt,
1 egg,
1 cup of water.

DIRECTIONS:—Beat egg up light; sift flour and baking powder together; add water to this; then the egg and salt; mix well and drop on top of chicken or meat that is boiling; cook a half an hour; do not have much water around them while cooking, as being under water makes them soggy.

BREAD PUDDING.

3 cups of bread crumbs,
1 cup of brown sugar,
1 pound of beef suet,
1 pound of raisins,
¼ pound of citron,
½ teaspoon of nutmeg,
9 eggs,
1 wine glass of brandy
½ cup of cream.
½ teaspoon of soda.

DIRECTIONS:—Wash the raisins and chop in a bowl with suet; first cutting suet with a little flour added to it; now add raisins, orange peel and citron; beat eggs light and put in bread crumbs, then the fruit, sugar, and nutmeg; add a pinch of salt; put brandy and cream in last. Beat well together and put in a pudding bag after being well flavored; boil four hours. Serve with any good sauce.

INDIAN MEAL PUDDING.

2 pints of sweet milk,
½ pint of suet,
1 teaspoon of soda,
1 pint of chopped apples,
1 teaspoon of cinnamon,
¼ teaspoon of salt,
1 cup of molasses.

DIRECTIONS:—Scald the milk; sift in enough meal to make a stiff batter; then add the chopped suet and apples; next add molasses with the soda dissolved in them.

GREEN CORN PUDDING.

6 ears of corn,
¼ cup of sugar,
¼ cup of butter,
4 teaspoons of flour,
3 teaspoons of salt,
1 pint of sweet milk,
1 teaspoon of pepper.

DIRECTIONS.—Cut corn from the cob; add the milk; stir the sugar and flour together; then add the butter, pepper and salt; grease a pan and put in to bake until well done; serve while very hot.

SNOW PUDDING.

1 cup of hot water,
2 tablespoons corn starch, moistened in a little cold water,
Whites of two eggs.

DIRECTIONS.—Beat eggs stiff; set pail in hot water, cook ten minutes; stir often; wet the cups in cold water, so that the pudding will turn out easily; divide equally; set on ice; it can be kept on ice two days; turn out on saucers, and pour the following custard around:

Yolks of two eggs,
⅔ cup of sugar,

Small bit of butter, beaten with ⅔ cup milk; make in a quart measure; set in hot water till it thickens, but not curdled; flavor with lemon or vanilla; pour around pudding and serve.

CORN STARCH PUDDING.

1 pint of milk,
2 large tablespoons of corn starch,
1 egg,
1 pinch of salt,
½ cup of sugar,
1 small teaspoon of lemon.

DIRECTIONS.—Heat the milk; beat the egg and stir in; add the sugar, salt and lemon; last the corn starch, dissolved in milk; cook till thick; then turn in a mold and let cool; serve with any tart sauce, or whipped cream.

GOLDEN PUDDING.

1 cup of sugar,
2 eggs,
Juice of one lemon,
1 cup of sweet milk,
4 tablespoons of butter,
2½ cups of flour,
2 teaspoons of baking powder.

DIRECTIONS.—Cream butter and sugar; beat eggs separately; add yolks with sugar and butter; beat well; add the flour by sifting in; have baking powder sifted in flour; last add juice of lemon; bake in shallow pans one-half an hour; serve with the following sauce:

2 tablespoons of butter,
1 small cup of sugar,
2 teaspoons of flour,
1 pint boiling water,
White of one egg,
1 teaspoon of lemon.

DIRECTIONS.—Beat butter and sugar; moisten flour with a little cold water; pour the hot water over and stir the beaten white of the egg in, and lemon: cook over boiling water.

YANKEE PUDDING.

5 eggs,
¾ of a box of gelatine,
1 pint of cold water.
1½ cups of white sugar,
1 teaspoon of vanilla.

DIRECTIONS:—Dissolve the gelatine in the cold water; add the sugar and the whites of the eggs whisked till very light; last the vanilla; pour into molds; make a custard of the yolks of the eggs by using one cup of sugar, one pint of sweet milk and one teaspoon of vanilla; cook till it thickens; let cool; turn the pudding out into a dish; pour over the custard and serve.

CORN STARCH PUDDING.

1 pint of rich milk,
½ cup of corn starch,
¼ teaspoon of salt,
½ cup of white sugar,
1 teaspoon of vanilla.

DIRECTIONS:—Scald the milk; whip the eggs light; put the sugar in; dissolve corn starch in a little milk; when the milk has reached the boiling point, stir in the corn starch; let cook till it thickens, then remove from the stove and flavor; pour into cups to mold; turn out in sauce dishes. Serve with whipped cream.

FROZEN PUDDING.

2 eggs,
1½ cups of flour,
2 cups of sugar,
1 large cup of milk,
2 tablespoons of gelatine,
1 quart of cream,
1 pound of candied fruit.

DIRECTIONS.—Let the milk come to a boil; mix the flour, eggs and sugar together and stir in the boiling milk; cook for fifteen minutes; then add the gelatine, after soaking it for three hours in water enough to cover it; set away to cool; then add the sugar and cream; freeze ten minutes; then add the candied fruits; then finish freezing; remove the dasher and beat up with a paddle; pack and set away for several hours; when ready to serve dip in hot water; turn into a glass dish; whip cream; put around with some candied fruits in it.

YORKSHIRE PUDDING.

¾ cup of sweet milk,
1 egg,
¼ cup of flour,
1 pinch of salt.

DIRECTIONS—Beat the egg till light colored and thick; add it to the milk; sift flour and salt and add enough to eggs to make a stiff paste; be sure the lumps are all out while it is in the thick state; then add the rest of the mixture and beat till smooth; pour in a brick shaped pan and bake one-half hour in a brisk oven; cut in squares and serve with roast beef on a hot plate.

WEST INDIA PUDDING.

½ of a good sized sponge cake,
1 pint of cream,
8 eggs,
½ cup of sugar,
2 ounces of preserved ginger.

DIRECTIONS:—Break the sponge cake up; scald cream and sweeten with the sugar; pour over the crumbs, cover till the cake is soaked; then add the eggs after being well beaten; butter a pudding mold and pour in the mixture; put pieces of ginger around the pudding; tie down with a cloth and steam for an hour and a half. Serve with the syrup the ginger has been in; pour over the pudding. This is nice hot or cold, whichever is desired. A good sauce for the pudding is:

1 cup of sugar,
½ cup of butter,
1 cup of boiling hot wine.

DIRECTIONS:—Whip to a foam; flavor with any flavoring desired, but the wine is all that is needed, as it gives a fine flavor.

CURRANT PUDDING.

1 quart of milk,
4 eggs,
1 cup of sugar,
2 cups of ripe currant juice.

DIRECTIONS:—Put milk, sugar and beaten eggs together; have several slices of stale bread; lay in a baking pan and pour over the custard of milk, sugar and eggs; bake in a moderate oven and pour over them the cups of juice with one cup of white sugar stirred into it and the whites of two eggs beaten stiff and dropped in hot water a moment and put over the top of the pudding before sending to the table.

BAKED APPLE DUMPLINGS.

3 cups of flour,
2 teaspoons of baking powder,
¼ teacup of butter,
¼ teaspoon of salt,
Whites of 2 eggs,
1 cup of milk,
8 large sized apples.
1 cup of sugar.

DIRECTIONS.—Put flour, after baking powder has been put into it, in a mixing bowl; add salt, butter and milk; rub the butter in the dry flour; beat the egg stiff and add; then the sugar; make out; roll in pieces large enough to cover one apple; put dumplings in a greased baking pan, and put enough sugar and butter in to season them nicely; add a little cinnamon; when they are done remove from pan and place on pie plates; serve with any good sauce.

BOILED DUMPLINGS, NO. 1.

6 good ripe apples,
½ cup of sour milk,
¼ teaspoon of soda,
¼ teaspoon of salt.
1 tablespoon of lard.

DIRECTIONS.—Sift flour into mixing bowl; put lard in; mix well in the flour; add salt and soda, disolved in the milk; make a stiff paste; roll out; pare the apples and halve them; put in crust and fasten them up—only a small place at top; put in small sacks; salt sacks is nice for them; flour inside; put in boiling water and cook until well done; then remove and serve while warm; eat with any good sauce.

STRAWBERRY PUDDING.

2 cups of milk.
4 eggs,
2 cups of cake crumbs,
1 small cup of sugar,
1 small cup of butter,
2 cups of strawberries.

DIRECTIONS.—Soak the cake crumbs in the milk; beat the butter and yolks of the eggs, and whites of two; then add to the milk; stir well together and bake some longer than thirty minutes; then pour the berries over the top, after cleaning and hulling; spread over this a meringue of the whites of the two eggs and one cup of sugar; flavor with vanilla; place in the oven a few moments; serve with cream.

PEACH DUMPLINGS.

Take as many ripe peaches as dumplings wanted; pare them and sprinkle sugar over them and let stand a few minutes; make a crust a little richer than biscuit dough; roll out about a quarter of an inch thick; put one peach to each piece of dough; roll over and pinch the dough together; add a small piece of butter and about one teaspoon of water to each dumpling; bake in a rather quick oven till well done; serve with any good sauce that is preferred.

PIES.

PUFF PASTE, FOR PIES OR PUDDINGS.

1 pound of butter,
1 pound of flour,
1 cup of ice water.

DIRECTIONS:—Have all the water out of the butter; divide in two parts; sift flour; divide same as the butter. Put the flour in a mixing bowl, chop one half of the butter in; now take the ice water and begin to mix butter with flour; add the water little at a time until all is used; now take out of bowl and lay on the molding board and roll out, and as you do this, keep adding a little of the remaining butter and flour; sprinkle on until all is used; turn over and roll together. This an excellent paste.

FLAKY PIE CRUST.

Use two tablespoons of lard and a sprinkle of salt to every pie; if the lard is very cold, warm a little and add to the flour; have the water cold, but not quite ice cold; mix with a spoon, as it makes it more flaky than to mix with the hands; do not knead more than possible. This will, if properly made, almost melt in the mouth.

OLDEN TIME PIE CRUST.

1 cup of lard,
1 cup of butter,
½ teaspoon of salt,
½ cup of sour milk,
¼ teaspoon of soda.

DIRECTIONS.—Sift flour into mixing bowl; cut the lard in; then the butter and salt; mix till powdered fine; add soda, dissolved in the sour milk; make a stiff dough; have the shortening and milk cold; this is very nice for all kinds of fruit pies, and for pudding also.

POTATO CRUST.

1 cup of mashed potatoes,
2 cups of milk,
2 tablespoons of butter,
1 teaspoon of baking powders.

DIRECTIONS.—Boil and mash potatoes; add this to the flour, then the butter chopped in; next add the milk slowly; sift the baking powders with some of the flour and add to the other; make as stiff as ordinary pie crust.

TO GLACE PIE CRUST.

1 egg,
1 teaspoon of sugar,

DIRECTIONS.—Beat the white of the egg; add the sugar. This is used to prevent any of the juice of fruit pies soaking in the crust, also improves the appearance of the tops of biscuits, rusks and ginger cakes.

CHICKEN PIE

1 good sized chicken,
½ cup of butter.

Cook chicken so it will fall from the bones; take out, cool and strip from the bones; then have a crust similar to biscuit dough only richer; line a good sized baking pan with a crust, then put in a layer of chicken, then some butter; now roll out some dough thin as possible; cut in small pieces; cover the layer of chicken; use butter, crust and chicken till all is used up; then take some of the gravy the chicken was cooked in and thicken it a little and pour over almost a teacupful; cover with strips of dough; send to the oven and bake slowly until well done.

MINCE MEAT.

5 pounds of chopped meat,
2 pounds of suet,
2 cups of raisins,
2 cups of currants,
½ pound of citron,
2 cups of brown sugar,
2 cups of molasses,
6 cups of chopped apples,
1 tablespoon of salt,
2 tablespoons of cinnamon,
1 nutmeg,
2 cups of chopped figs,
1 tablespoon of cloves,
1 tablespoon of spice,
1 quart of cider,
1 pint of brandy.

DIRECTIONS:—Cook meat very tender; get beef neck, as it makes nicer pies than any other part of the beef; chop suet and fruit, after seeding the raisins and cleaning the currants; add the fruit to the meat and suet; then the spices; next the sugar, molasses, brandy and cider. If you prefer, the brandy may be omitted, but with it the meat will keep longer. Grate the nutmeg in; add the salt. This will be a large enough quantity for an ordinary sized family. This very rich and nice.

MINCE PIE.

1 cup of good mince meat,
¼ cup of sugar,
2 tablespoons of water.

DIRECTIONS.—Have a nice light pie crust, line a pie tin; put the meat in; put sugar and water on top of meat; have two crusts; bake not too brown, unless, needed right away, as they will be warmed before serving.

GREEN TOMATO PIE.

3 medium sized tomatoes,
1 cup of sugar,
1 orange,
1 tablespoon of butter,
1 sprinkle of cinnamon,
½ cup of chopped raisins.

DIRECTIONS.—Slice the tomatoes very thin; line a pie tin with rich crust; put the tomatoes and raisins in; sprinkle the sugar over; add the butter, cinnamon and juice of the orange; bake with an upper crust.

PIE PLANT PIE.

1 large cup of sliced pie plant,
1 cup of sugar,
1 tablespoon of butter,
1 tablespoon of flour.

DIRECTIONS:—Slice pie plant round ways; make a good crust; add the flour to sugar and put the pie plant in them; sprinkle sugar and flour over it; bake with upper crust; at first bake rather slow, until the pie plant has time to cook and extract the juice, as no water is put in this pie.

BLACK BERRY PIE.

1 pint of berries,
1½ cups of sugar,
1 teaspoon of flour.

DIRECTIONS.—Have crust same as other berry pies; roll out; line a pie tin and put berries in, after being washed and drained of all the water; add flour to the sugar; sprinkle over the berries; bake with an upper crust; do not put any water in unless berries are not very ripe, then only about one tablespoonful.

PINEAPPLE PIE

½ of a pineapple,
1 cup of white sugar,
1 tablespoon of lemon juice,
1 tablespoon of brandy.

DIRECTIONS.—Pare and grate the pineapple; add sugar and lemon juice; then roll your crust out and put in pie tin; put in and cover with strips of the paste; bake in a rather quick oven; add brandy last; serve with creamy sauce.

LEMON FRUIT PIE.

1 cup of raisins,
1 lemon,
1 cup of sugar,
1 tablespoon of butter,
3 tablespoons of water.

DIRECTIONS.—Stone and chop the raisins; use pulp and juice of the lemon; bake with two crusts; this is very nice and as rich as mince pie.

SQUASH PIE.

½ pint of squash,
½ cup of white sugar,
1 tablespoon of butter,
1 cup of sweet milk,
1 egg,
1 teaspoon of cinnamon.

DIRECTIONS:—Bake any good, mealy squash. After baking scrape the meat from the rind; add beaten eggs, sugar and milk; butter and cinnamon; beat well. Any other spices or flavoring may be used. Bake with an under crust; brown nicely on top. The pie is better if a little sugar and butter is put on top before sending to the oven. Sprinkle some cinnamon on, too, it will brown nicer.

SLICED APPLE PIE.

2 good sized apples.
1 cup of white sugar,
1 tablespoon of flour,
1 tablespoon of butter,
¼ teaspoon of nutmeg,
¼ cup of hot water.

DIRECTIONS:—Slice apples very thin; make a crust very light and rich; roll out moderately thick; put in a good sized pie tin; put apples in, sprinkle sugar in with the flour—mixed with it, next the butter cut into pieces, now nutmeg and hot water; make with an upper crust; bake rather fast.

MOCK MINCE MEAT.

8 crackers,
¼ cup of butter,
1 cup of molasses,
1 cup of sugar,
1¼ cups of cider,
½ cup of raisins,
½ cup of currants,
½ teaspoon of spice,
1½ teaspoons of cinnamon.

DIRECTIONS:—Put butter, molasses, cider, and crackers mashed fine, together; seed raisins, clean currants; add them and the spices; cook about twenty minutes; remove from the stove and keep in a cool place. This will make a number of pies.

PRESERVE PIE.

1 cup of any kind of preserves.
½ cup of thick sweet cream,
¼ cup of butter,
2 eggs,
½ cup of sugar,
1 tablespoon of flour.

DIRECTIONS:—Make a nice crust; line a deep pie tin; mix the preserves, butter and sugar with the flour; then beat the yolks of the eggs light and add to the cream, beat all well together; then put in the tins and bake rather quick; ice with the whites of the eggs and a half a cup of sugar; flavor with some good tart jelly; ice and set in the stove a few minutes.

COCOANUT PIE, NO. 2.

½ cocanut, grated,
2 eggs,
1½ cups of sugar,
¼ cup of butter,
½ cup of milk.

DIRECTIONS.—Grate cocoanut; rub butter and sugar together; add the eggs, beaten separately; next the milk; last the cocoanut sprinkled in; bake with one crust; ice on top.

PUMPKIN PIE.

1 cup of pumpkin,
1 small cup of sugar,
1 cup of sweet cream,
2 eggs,
1 teaspoon of cinnamon.

DIRECTIONS.—Cook pumpkin well; pass through a colander; beat whites of the eggs separate from the yolks; add yolks and white of one egg, sugar and cinnamon; last cream; bake with an under crust; ice with the white of the egg left; put in oven and brown slightly.

VINEGAR PIE.

1 tablespoon of butter,
½ cup of vinegar,
½ cup of hot water,
1½ cup of sugar,
1 egg,
1 teaspoon of flour,
1 teaspoon of lemon extract,

DIRECTIONS.—Put vinegar and water together; then add sugar and flour, mixed together; then the butter and beaten egg; set over hot water and cook till it thickens; remove from stove and flavor with lemon; line pie tins with puff paste and pour the mixture in; bake with an under crust.

COCOANUT PIE, NO 1.

1 cup of grated cocoanut,
1 cup of white sugar,
Whites of four eggs,
4 tablespoons of good cream,
2 tablespoons of butter,
1 teaspoon rose extract.

DIRECTIONS.—Beat the sugar and butter; add the cocoanut, cream and rose extract, a little at a time; beat the whites stiff; add them, beating very light; bake with an under crust in a rather quick oven.

LEMON TARTS.

3 lemons,
1 cup of water,
½ cup of blanched almonds,
2 cups of sugar,
1 tablespoon of flour,
1 tablespoon of butter.

DIRECTIONS.—Pare lemons, roll them and press out the juice; have a sharp knife; cut the lemon up; add the juice and sugar with the flour; add butter and blanched, chopped almonds last; cook till thick; have some tart pans lined with good crust; fill with the filling and bake; put currant jelly on top, when cool.

LEMON PIE NO. 1.

1 cup of water,
1 cup of white sugar,
2 teaspoonfuls corn starch,
Yolks of two eggs,
Rind and juice of 2 lemons.

DIRECTIONS.—Place water and sugar on stove; when it boils thirken with the corn starch; take from the fire and stir in yolks of eggs, well beaten, and the grated rind and juice of the lemons; bake the crust partly; then fill and bake till done; ice and set in oven till brown. This is excellent.

LEMON PIE, NO. 2.

1 cup of cream,
1 cup of sugar,
1 tablespoon of flour,
Whites of 2 eggs,
Juice of 2 lemons,
Rind of 1 lemon,

DIRECTIONS:—Sift sugar and flour together, add this to the juice of the lemons, then stir in the cream and eggs beaten well; heat over boiling water till it cooks and begins to thicken, then remove and grate in the rind, and bake with an under crust. Remove when done, and beat one egg with one-half cup of sugar, and spread on top of pie. Return to the stove; brown slightly.

LEMON PIE, NO. 3.

1 cup of white sugar,
1 tablespoon of butter,
1 egg,
1 lemon,
1 teacup of hot water,
1 tablespoon of corn starch.

DIRECTIONS:—Dissolve corn starch in cold water, then stir in the hot water, cream, butter and sugar; pour over the hot mixture. When cold add the lemon juice, rind, and egg well beaten. Bake without an upper crust.

LEMON PIE, NO. 4.

1 tablespoon of butter,
2 cups of sugar,
4 eggs,
Juice and rind of 2 lemons,
1 teacup of milk.

DIRECTIONS:—Cream the butter and sugar together; add lemon juice, then the milk, after this grated rind of the lemon. This will make two pies in large pans. To be baked with an under crust.

BANANNA PIE.

3 good sized banannas,
1 cup of cream,
1 tablespoon of orange juice,
½ cup of white sugar.

DIRECTIONS:—Make a rich crust; line pan and slice the banannas thin; put in pan, then sprinkle sugar over; then beat cream up, but do not whip it; pour over, and last add the orange juice; bake and cover with a meringue made with the whites of two eggs, one half cup of sugar; flavor with orange juice; spread on top and set in the oven to brown.

FRIED PEACH PIE.

1 pint of stewed peaches,
½ cup of sugar,
Flavor with nutmeg.

DIRECTIONS:—Make a crust a little richer than biscuit dough, but have it light; roll out and cut in pieces about the size of saucers; mash the peaches; add the sugar and put about two tablespoons on each pie; roll over and fry in hot grease until a nice brown. To be eaten with cream or sauce.

CRANBERRY PIE.

1 pint of cranberries, mashed fine,
1 large cup of sugar,
1 tablespoon of butter.

DIRECTIONS:—Put cranberries in a sauce pan; put in about one half cup of hot water and the sugar and butter; stew till well done; then remove from the fire and have a crust ready baked; mash fine and put in the pan and sprinkle a little powdered sugar over top and return to the oven a few minutes.

CREAM RASPBERRY TARTS.

1 quart ripe berries,
1 cup of white sugar,
1 cup cream,
Whites of two eggs.
1 teaspoon of flour.

DIRECTIONS.—Make a nice, rich puff paste; pick berries; wash and drain; roll out paste and put in tart shells; put top on and bake; remove top and put the berries in, and put cream, flour and sugar together; cook till it thickens; then beat the whites of the eggs to a stiff froth; stir in; lift top and pour in and serve.

HAM PATTIES.

Make a rather rich dough for crusts; line patty pans; fill in with cold boiled ham, cut in small pieces; fill the pans and pour over the following: Make a rich gravy, by putting some butter in a frying pan and add some flour; let brown, and put enough cream in to make it as thick as desired, then salt and pepper; cover the meat with this and put a top crust on; send to the oven and cook till the crust is well done; serve at once, or it is nice cold and warmed over in a slow oven.

APPLE PIE WITH MERRINGUE.

1 pint of mashed apples,
1 small cup of sugar,
1 tablespoon of butter,
1 teaspoon of lemom juice.

DIRECTIONS.—Cook good tart apples well done; remove from kettle and press through a colander; add butter, sugar and lemon juice; bake with an under crust; merringue for top is made with one egg, well beaten, one-fourth cup of sugar, one-fourth teaspoon of lemon; put this on top of pie; set in oven a few minutes till a light brown.

LUNCHEON PATTIES.

1 pound of boiled chicken,
1 can of mushrooms,
1 cup chicken gravy,
1 cup of milk,
1 tablespoon of flour,
1 tablespoon of butter,
1 teaspoon of salt,
½ teaspoon of pepper,
1 lemon.

DIRECTIONS:—Boil the chicken until very tender; chop fine; add the mushrooms after being removed from the liquor in the can; add the gravy, salt and pepper; boil the milk and thicken with the flour; now add the butter, last the lemon juice; mix well; put in a pan and heat well, but do not let it boil. Fill dainty patty shells and it is ready to serve.

RASPBERRY TARTS AND CREAM.

1 quart of ripe berries,
1 pint of white sugar,
Whites of two eggs,
1 pint of cream.

DIRECTIONS:—Make a nice puff paste; line the tins and bake; take out and have the berries mashed and sugar and cream added and fill in; beat the whites of the eggs to a stiff froth, add one half a cup of sugar and one teaspoon of rose extract; spread on top and put in the oven only a minute; do not let brown too much. Serve with whipped cream or any good sauce.

CREAM PIE, NO. 1.

1 cup of sugar,
1 cup of flour,
1 teaspoon of cream of tartar,
½ teaspoon of soda,
3 eggs,
1 teaspoon of lemon extract.

DIRECTIONS.—Beat eggs separately; add sugar lightly, with the yolks of the eggs; sift flour, cream of tartar and soda three times, add the whites; then sift in flour lightly; last add flavoring; put in jelly cake tins and bake in a quick oven; be sure and line the tins with paper; take out of pans and let cool; add the following filling: 2 eggs, 1 cup of sugar, ½ cup of flour, 1 pint of cream, 1 teaspoon of lemon; beat eggs light; add cream; then sugar and flour mixed together; set in boiling water to cook; when thick remove from stove; when partly cold add lemon; fill in between layers.

CREAM PIE, NO. 2.

5 eggs,
1 cup of flour,
1 cup of white sugar,
1 teaspoon of baking powder.

DIRECTIONS.—Beat eggs separately; add flour and sugar, together, after baking powder has been sifted in; sift this in the eggs; mix up quickly, and make three layers; use the following filling: 1 pint of whipped cream, 1 teaspoon of vanilla, ½ cup of sugar; whip cream very stiff; add sugar lightly; and flavoring last; mix; then after the layers have cooled, put between layers, and on top; serve immediately, or if liked, it will improve it by setting on ice a few minutes. This is very nice.

GRAPE PIE.

1 pint of ripe grapes,
1 cup of sugar,
2 good sized crackers,
1 tablespoon of thick cream.

DIRECTIONS:—Remove seeds from the grapes; line a pie tin with light rich crust; put in grapes, then sugar and crackers, pounded fine. Bake with strips on top.

TARLATAN PIE.

½ cup of cream.
1 cup of sugar,
1 cup of apples,
1 egg,
2 teaspoons of lemon juice.

DIRECTIONS:—Stew apples tender; pass through a colander; add the cream, beaten egg, and sugar; next the lemon. Bake with one crust and serve with cream.

PRUNE PIE.

1 cup of prunes,
1 cup of sugar,
½ cup of boiled cider.

DIRECTIONS:—Cook prunes done; remove the pits; mash fine and add sugar and boiled cider; make a nice crust; put in the mixture and put on an upper crust and bake in a moderate oven.

PEACH COBBLER.

1 dozen ripe peaches,
2 cups of white sugar,
½ cup of hot water.

DIRECTIONS:—Pare and slice the peaches; lay on a plate and sprinkle sugar over; take a nice rich pie dough; roll out same as for any other pie; line a deep pie dish; put in some peaches; then thin slices of the dough; then another layer of peaches and dough till all is used; cover top with crust. Just before sending to the oven, put a half a cup of hot water in and bake in a moderate oven, as the under and top crusts will be done before the peaches and inside dough are done. Serve with good cream. This makes a large pie.

IRISH POTATO PIE.

2 good sized potatoes,
1 pint sweet milk,
2 tablespoons of butter,
3 eggs,
½ glass good brandy,
¼ teaspoon of nutmeg,
½ cup of sugar.

DIRECTIONS:—Grate the potato; add butter and sugar beaten well together; then the milk and yolks of the eggs and the white of one; reserve the other two whites for frosting; add brandy and nutmeg just before putting in the oven; bake with an under crust in a quick oven; ice with one small cup of sugar and the whites of the two eggs and flavor with lemon. Spread on top and set in the oven till a nice brown.

RASPBERRY PIE.

1 pint of berries,
1 cup of white sugar,
2 tablespoons of hot water,
1 tablespoon of butter,
1 teaspoon of flour.

DIRECTIONS.—Take nice, ripe berries; wash them and drain; have a nice crust; mix flour and sugar together; add this to the berries; stir together; then put in the pie; add butter and water; bake with a top crust.

APPLE TARTS.

1 pint of mashed apples,
¼ cup of cream,
1 cup of sugar,
1 tablespoon of butter,
1 teaspoon of cinnamon.

DIRECTIONS.—Cook apples well; mash fine; add sugar, cream and butter; last cinnamon; mix all well together; roll out your paste and line tart pans; fill in the mixture and bake in a quick oven; after removing from stove, sprinkle some sugar over the top; any good jelly may be put over them if desired.

DATE AND APPLE PIE.

1 cup of dates,
1 cup of chopped apples,
½ cup of sugar,
¼ cup of water.

DIRECTIONS.—Stone the dates; chop the apples fine; add the sugar and water; bake with two crusts.

CURRANT PIE.

1 pint of currants,
2 small cups of sugar,
1 tablespoon of flour,
1 tablespoon of water.

DIRECTIONS:—Pick the currants from the stems and wash them; line a pie tin with a rich crust; put currants in and add sugar, flour and water; have two crusts; bake in a quick oven, as currants are easily cooked and if baked slow the juice will soak in the crust.

CHICKEN TARTS.

1 cup of chopped chicken,
1 cup of rich gravy,
¼ teaspoon of pepper,
1 tablespoon of butter.

DIRECTIONS:—Make a rich puff paste; chop the chicken; any other meats can be substituted for the chicken; add pepper and butter; salt while cooking, as it imparts a better flavor; pour in the gravy, roll paste out and bake in small pans until the gravy is mixed well with the chicken.

PEACH PIE.

1 large cup of ripe peaches,
1 cup of white sugar.

DIRECTIONS:—Make a rich crust; roll and bake in a pie tin, quick, but a nice brown, put one layer in the tin and grease it slightly with butter, and put the other layer on top; when nicely browned remove from the oven; separate and put cup of peaches with the sugar and fill in and put top on again and serve with whipped cream.

CANNED PEACH PIE.

1 can of peaches,
1½ cups of sugar,
1 tablespoon of flour.

DIRECTIONS:—Make a rich crust; line a pie tin; slice peaches; put in; add the flour to sugar and sprinkle over the peaches; put in some of the syrup from the peaches; bake with two crusts; this makes two pies.

SWEET POTATO PIE.

1 large sweet potato,
½ cup of white sugar,
1 tablespoon of butter,
1 teaspoon of cinnamon,
¼ cup of cream.

DIRECTIONS.—Cook potatoes till well done; slice thin; make a good crust; put in a pie tin; put the sliced potato in; cut the butter and add to it; next put sugar in, and cream and cinnamon; bake with an upper crust or without, whichever is preferred.

STRAWBERRY PIE.

1 pint of nice large berries,
1 cup of white sugar,
1 cup of good cream.

DIRECTIONS.—Make a rich crust; line a pie tin; bake in a quick oven; take out and have berries picked and washed; put sugar over them; stir up and put in the tin; whip the cream and put over the top of pie; put on ice at least one-half an hour before serving.

LEMON POTATO PIE.

1 cup of sugar,
1 large Irish potato,
½ cup of water,
1 lemon,
¼ cup of butter,
1 tablespoon of flour.

DIRECTIONS:—Grate the potato; add sugar, butter, and juice of the lemon and grated rind; now the water and flour; rub butter and flour together. Bake with two crusts.

ORANGE TART.

3 large oranges,
1½ cups of sugar,
1 tablespoon of butter,
½ cup of water.

DIRECTIONS:—Squeeze juice and pulp from the oranges; add the sugar, butter and water; put in a kettle, cook till it thickens; pour out and bake crust as usual for tarts, fill with with the mixture; ice the top of them; set in the oven a few minutes till a delicate brown.

RIPE TOMATO PIE.

3 good sized tomatoes,
1 cup of brown sugar,
½ cup of cream,
1 tablespoon of flour.
¼ teaspoon of nutmeg.

DIRECTIONS:—Slice tomatoes, line a pie tin with good rich paste; put tomatoes in, then add the flour to the sugar and put in; last, the cream and nutmeg. Bake with two crusts in a moderate oven.

CHERRY PIE.

1 pint of ripe cherries.
1½ cups of white sugar,
1 tablespoon of butter.

DIRECTIONS.—Remove the pits; make a nice puff paste; line a deep pie plate; squeeze all the juice out of cherries that you can; then put cherries, and the sugar and butter in; set in the oven and bake till well done. Do not have oven too hot, or the crust will be done before the cherries.

JELLY PIE.

1 glass of any good jelly,
1 pint of thick cream,
1 cup of sugar,
1 teaspoon of vanilla.

DIRECTIONS.—Make a very light, rich crust; line tart shells; beat jelly up well. This will make about six tarts, if a common sized glass of jelly is used. Whip the cream stiff; flavor and sweeten with sugar; after they have been baked, put the jelly in; then the whipped cream on top; send to the table immediately.

GOOSEBERRY PIE.

1 pint of gooseberries,
1½ cup sof sugar,
1 tablespoon of flour,
1 tablespoon of butter.

DIRECTIONS.—Take light, rich pie dough and line pie tins; stew berries and put in the pies; add flour to sugar; sift in last; add butter; then put top on pie and bake quickly, to a nice brown. Sometimes a pinch of soda added when berries are put in, takes that sharp, acid taste from them.

CRANBERRY AND RAISIN PIE.

1 cup of cranberries,
½ cup of raisins,
1 cup of sugar,
2 tablespoons of water,
1 tablespoon of flour,
1 tablespoon of butter.

DIRECTIONS.—Pick and stone the raisins; wash the cranberries; have a nice crust made; roll out and sprinkle with flour; add raisins, cranberries and sugar, with flour mixed in it; last add butter; do not use only the two tablespoons of water; bake with two crusts.

OYSTER PIE.

1 can of fresh oysters,
1 egg,
1 cup of powdered crackers,
1 teaspoon of pepper,
1 teaspoon of salt,
1 tablespoon of butter.

DIRECTIONS.—Make a nice, rich crust; line a pan, and put some oysters in; then a layer of crackers; then oysters, etc., till all is used; beat egg light; add to the liquor, the egg, pepper, salt and butter; heat and pour over the other mixture in the pan; put a top crust on and bake in a quick oven.

SUGAR PIE.

1 cup of brown sugar,
½ cup of butter,
1 tablespoon of flour,
1 teaspoon of lemon extract,
2 eggs,
¼ cup of cream.

DIRECTIONS.—Whip the eggs well; add the butter and flour; mix together, and add the cream and flavoring; bake with an under crust; ice the top if preferred. It is excellent.

CHOCOLATE PIE.

1 cup of cream,
¼ cup of flour,
1 cup of sugar,
1 teaspoon of vanilla,
2 eggs,
¼ cup of grated chocolate.

DIRECTIONS.—Heat the cream; mix the flour with the sugar and add; whip the yolks of the eggs light and add them; cook a few minutes and add the chocolate; last the flavoring; make a rich paste and line a tin and pour the filling in; bake in a rather quick oven, as the filling is already cooked; ice the top with the whites of the two eggs. This makes a large pie and is very rich.

Layer Cakes.

APPLE SHORT CAKE.

1 cup of sugar,
¾ cup of butter,
½ cup of milk,
2 cups of flour,
1 teaspoon of cream of tartar,
½ teaspoon of soda.

DIRECTIONS:—Mix as other cakes and bake in jelly tins.

FILLING.

3 large apples,
1 egg,
1 cup of sugar,
1 lemon.

Directions for filling:—Grate the apples; beat the egg; add juice and grated rind of the lemon; let come to a boil; spread between layers of cake.

JELLY CAKE ROLL.

1½ cups of white sugar,   2 eggs,
2 cups of flour,   1 teaspoon of lemon.
2 small teaspoons of baking powder.

DIRECTIONS:—Beat eggs well together; add sugar and mix well; now sift in flour and baking powder sifted together; add flavoring; bake in a bread pan; line with paper; remove from pan and when cooled a little, spread with any good jelly and roll up. Ice with one egg, 1 cup of pulverized sugar; flavor with lemon. Before putting on cake, put one tablespoon of jelly in the icing and spread over the rolls. Serve with whipped cream.

PINE APPLE SHORT CAKE.

2 tablespoons of butter,
2 tablespoons of sugar,
4 tablespoons of sweet milk,
1 egg,
½ cup of flour,
1 teaspoon of baking powder.

DIRECTIONS:—Beat butter, sugar and eggs together; add milk and flour with the baking powder sifted in; bake in a deep jelly tin; when done, cool and split in the centre and add the following filling: Slice very thin some canned pine apples; have about a cupful after sliced; lay this between cake and sprinkle with sugar. For the top take white of one egg; ½ cup of loaf sugar; 2 tablespoons of pine apple juice; beat till stiff; put on top of cake and send to the table immediately. Serve with whipped cream or any sauce.

AUTUMN CAKE.

2 cups of granulated sugar,
1 small cup of butter.
1 cup of cold water,
3½ cups of flour,
Whites of 7 eggs,
2 teaspoons of baking powder,
1 teaspoon of strawberry flavoring.

DIRECTIONS:—Mix butter and sugar together, add the cup of of water and one half of the flour; beat this a few minutes; then sift in the remaining flour with the baking powder; next add the whites beaten stiff; add a little at a time; last the flavoring. Make icing with 1 cup of loaf sugar, whites of 2 eggs beaten together stiff, then spread on layers and put currant jelly over this, then take some plain icing and put in two tablespoons chocolate; put over the currant jelly. This gives the autumnal effect.

CHOCOLATE CAKE, NO. 2.

2 cups of white sugar,
4 eggs,
1 cup of sweet milk,
3 cups of flour,
1 teaspoon of vanilla,
2 teaspoons of baking powder.

DIRECTIONS.—Cream butter, sugar and yolks of the eggs together; add milk and flour; next whites of eggs, beaten well; last baking powder, sifted in a little flour; bake in jelly tins, very soft.

DIRECTIONS FOR FILLING: Whites of three eggs, beaten stiff, two cups of pulverized sugar, one cake of chocolate, one teaspoon of vanilla; beat eggs; add sugar; grate the chocolate in and add flavoring; then spread between layers and on top of cake.

CHOCOLATE CARAMEL CAKE, NO. 1.

½ cup of butter,
1 large cup of sugar,
Yolks of 6 eggs,
⅔ cup of cream,
3 cups of flour,
2 teaspoons baking powder.

DIRECTIONS.—Beat butter, sugar and yolks for five minutes; then add some sifted flour, with baking powder sifted several times into it.

FILLING: 1 cake of chocolate, 1 tablespoon of butter, 1 cup of sweet cream, ½ cup of brown sugar.

DIRECTIONS.—Grate chocolate and add to cream, and butter and sugar, cooked over the fire till it is boiling, and seems sticky; remove from fire and beat thoroughly, and put between layers of cake; have three layers. This is excellent.

CARAMEL CAKE, NO. 2.

1 cup of butter,
2 cups of sugar,
1 cup of sweet milk,
1 cup of corn starch,
Whites of six eggs,
2 cups of flour,
2 tablespoons of baking powder,
1 teaspoon of vanilla.

DIRECTIONS:—Cream butter and sugar together; add some milk and flour alternately till all the flour is used; stir the beaten whites in next; then corn starch with baking powder; last vanilla; beat all ten minutes; bake in jelly tins, quick and soft.

FILLING:—One cup of white sugar; one-third cup of cold water; one-fourth cup of butter; one teaspoon of vanilla; boil five minutes without stirring; remove from the fire and stir till white and creamy but not too hard; put between layers and on top. It must be done quickly as it hardens very fast.

CARAMEL CAKE, NO. 3.

2 cups of sugar,
1 cup of butter,
1 cup of milk,
4 cups of flour,
1 teaspoon of vanilla,
Whites of 6 eggs,
2 teaspoons of baking powder.

DIRECTIONS:—Cream sugar and butter, add milk and two cups of flour; next add whites of the eggs and remaining flour, with baking powder sifted into it; bake in jelly tins, in a quick oven; let partly cool, have filling ready, spread between and on top of cake and ice, covering on top and sides. FILLING—Two cups of brown sugar, one cup of milk, one tablespoon of butter, two teaspoons of vanilla. Put butter, sugar, and milk in a sauce pan cook till thick; remove and beat till cool; add vanilla last.

NEW ORLEANS CHOCOLATE CAKE.

½ cup of butter,
2 small cups of loaf sugar,
1 cup of milk,
2 cups of flour,
4 eggs,
2 teaspoons of baking powder,
1 teaspoon of lemon extract,
½ cake of Baker's chocolate.

DIRECTIONS.—Cream the butter and sugar together; then add the milk and one cup of flour alternately; sift the baking powder and grated chocolate with the remaining cup of flour two or three times; last add the whites of the eggs; mix well and put in buttered tins, bake quick and soft; put together with cooked icing; for the top put some grated chocolate in the icing, but have it as white as possible on the sides. This is a very pretty cake as well as nice.

STRAWBERRY SHORT CAKE, NO. 1.

1 quart of flour,
1 pint of cream,
1½ cups of white sugar,
1 teaspoon of soda,
2 teaspoons of cream of tartar.

DIRECTIONS:—Mix by stirring in and out, not round and round; before the flour is all mixed in turn out on board, divide the dough, roll out one half and butter it, roll the other half and lay it evenly over this; bake quick as possible without burning; sweeten the berries and have them ready to spread on; as soon as the cakes comes from the oven, lift off the top, put the berries on the under part, turn the crust side down next to the berries, fill the top; set in the oven five minutes; have prepared whipped cream, pour this over just as sent to the table, after cutting in slices.

STRAWBERRY SHORT CAKE, NO. 2.

2 cups of flour,
1½ teaspoons of baking powder,
¼ cup of butter,
¼ cup of milk,
½ cup of white sugar.

DIRECTIONS:—Sift the flour and baking powder together; add butter cold, and mix thoroughly with the flour; then add milk to sugar, and make a stiff paste; roll out about one-fourth of an inch thick, put in a pie tin one layer over the other; bake quick; remove from pan, spread with butter; prepare berries by stemming and washing them, and lay in a colander to drain; spread on layers and sprinkle sugar thick over them and send to table immediately, as juice will spoil crust if allowed to stand long. For sauce use one cup of cream, 1 teaspoon of flour, one cup of sugar; sift sugar and flour together, set over boiling water and cook; remove and put one-half cup of berry juice in it; pour over cake and serve.

JELLY CAKE.

½ lb of butter,
½ lb of sugar,
5 eggs,
6 oz. of flour,
3 oz. of corn starch,
1 teaspoon of vanilla,
1 cup of milk,
1 teaspoon of soda,
2 teaspoons of cream of tartar.

DIRECTIONS:—Beat butter, sugar and yolks light; add milk and some flour; dissolve soda in the milk, then add the whites stiffly beaten, and the remaining flour with cream of tartar, sifted four times; last, the vanilla. Bake in jelly tins, quick and soft. Spread between layers, with any good jelly, and ice on top and sides with whites of two eggs, one cup of confectioners' sugar, and flavor with same as the cake. This is delicious if properly made.

LEMON CAKE.

1½ cups of sugar,
½ cup of butter,
2½ cups of flour,
½ cup of sweet milk,
6 eggs, beaten separately,
2 teaspoons baking powder, or 1 of soda and 2 cream tartar.

DIRECTIONS:—Cream butter and sugar together; add milk and one-half of the flour and beaten yolks of the eggs; beat this ten minutes, then add the whites and remainder of the flour, with baking powder sifted into it; bake quick and soft.

FILLING—1 cup of hot water, 1½ cups of sugar, two tablespoons of flour; mix with the sugar one egg beaten and added to sugar, water and flour, juice of 1 large lemon, and a little of the rind grated; boil till it thickens, let it cool and then spread between the layers.

GOLDEN CREAM CAKE.

1 cup of butter,
1 cup of sugar,
1 cup of sweet milk,
2½ cups of flour,
Whites of 5 eggs,
1 teaspoon of soda,
2 teaspoons cream of tartar,
1 teaspoon of lemon.

DIRECTIONS:—Beat butter and sugar together for a few minutes, then add some of the milk and flour; leave one cup of the flour to sift cream of tartar in; add the whites of eggs beaten stiff, then the remaining cup of flour and flavoring; last, add soda dissolved in a little warm water; bake in jelly tins.

FILLING:—1 cup of sugar, 3 yolks of eggs, ½ cup of good cream, 1 teaspoon of corn starch. Cook in a tin pan set in hot water; moisten starch in the milk; cook till thick; flavor with orange; beat yolks and sugar, add to the cream and starch; spread between layers and on top, with yellow icing.

PECAN CREAM CAKE.

1½ cups of white sugar,
2½ cups of flour,
¼ cup of butter,
½ cup of sweet cream,
1 teaspoon of almond flavoring,
1 teaspoon of cream of tartar,
½ teaspoon of soda.

DIRECTIONS:—Beat yolks well; cream butter and sugar; next add flour with cream of tartar sifted twice through it; add flavoring and bake in jelly tins. Remove and let cool and spread the filling between and on top but not on sides of cake. Hull and chop pecan meats fine; cook one cup of cream and one tablespoon of flour till thick; add one cup of sugar and the pecan meats; when almost cold spread between and on top of the cake.

RAISIN CAKE.

2 cups of sugar,
1 cup of butter,
Whites of 4 eggs,
⅔ cup of milk,
3 cups of flour,
2 teaspoons of baking powder.

DIRECTIONS:—Mix cream, sugar and butter; add milk and two cups of flour; next the beaten whites and one cup of flour, with baking powder. Bake in jelly tins, quick and soft; flavor with lemon or vanilla if liked, or use raisins as flavoring.

FILLING—One cup of sugar, two whites of eggs, one teacup of raisins; cook sugar till thick, do not stir, pour over the beaten whites of eggs; stir in the chopped raisins; spread between layers.

MARSHMALLOW CAKE, NO. 1.

¼ pound of butter,
1½ cups of granulated sugar,
1 cup of water,
3 cups of flour,
2 teaspoons of baking powder,
Whites of 5 eggs.

Filling for Cake:
1 ounce of powdered gum arabic,
4 tablespoons of cold water,
4 ounces powdered sugar,
1 teaspoon of vanilla,
Whites of three eggs.

Directions.—Cream butter and sugar; next add a little water and flour, till two cups of flour is used, and all of the water; then add whites of eggs, stiffly beaten, and one-third cup of flour, with baking powder.

Directions for Filling.—Put gum arabic in a cup, and add four tablespoons of cold water; let stand half an hour; set in boiling water; stir till dissolved; strain through a cloth, and put in tin pail; set in boiling water, add the sugar; stir steadily and keep boiling for twenty minutes; then remove from the stove, and beat till white and stiff; set over fire again till scalding hot; remove and whip quickly; add a teaspoon of vanilla and the beaten whites of two eggs; set away in a cool place; when thoroughly cold, and cake cold also, spread this between layers of the cake, but have other icing for top and sides of cake. The water in which it is cooked must be kept boiling, and have eggs ready when needed.

To make a chocolate filling for this cake: Take the whites of two eggs, one and one-half cups of sugar, two tablespoons of cold water; beat this to a foam; then whip in lightly, six tablespoons of grated chocolate, and one teaspoon of vanilla; reserve a part to ice the top; spread the rest on the marshmallow filling; then stack the layers into a loaf. This makes a beautiful cake.

MARSHMALLOW CAKE, NO. 2.

1½ cups of sugar,
½ cup of butter,
½ cup of sweet milk,
1½ cups of flour,
½ cup of corn starch,
1 heaping teaspoon of baking powder,
Whites of six eggs.

DIRECTIONS.—Beat butter and sugar together; add one-half of the flour and then milk and baking powder sifted in the remainder of the flour and corn starch; last whip the eggs light and add. FILLING—2 tablespoons of gelatine, 8 tablespoons of hot water, 1 ℔ of loaf sugar, 1 teaspoon of vanilla. Dissolve the gelatine in the water, have it hot, stir the sugar in, stir half an hour and place in two tins the same size the cake was baked in; let mold and put between the layers.

CHOCOLATE MARSHMALLOW CAKE, NO. 3.

2 cups of loaf sugar,
½ cup of butter,
1 cup of cream,
3 cups of flour,
2 teaspoons of baking powder,
1 teaspoon of vanilla,
Whites of 5 eggs.

DIRECTIONS:—Cream the butter; add the sugar and beat five minutes; then add the cream and flour a little at a time; then baking powder sifted in one cup of flour; add the eggs whipped light; then the cup of flour with the baking powder; last the eggs and vanilla. FILLING—Whites of 2 eggs, ½ cup of loaf sugar, 2 tablespoons cold water, 6 tablespoons of chocolate, 1 teaspoon of vanilla. Put whites of eggs, sugar and water together, beat till stiff; then add the grated chocolate; divide this into four parts, put on layers on top of marshmallow filling. Marsh filling made same as Marshmallow, No. 2.

BLACKBERRY CAKE.

½ cup of butter,
4 eggs,
2 cups of flour,
1½ cups of white sugar,
1 cup of blackberry preserves,
4 tablespoons of sweet cream,
¼ teaspoon of soda,
1 small teaspoon of cream of tartar,
1 teaspoon of cinnamon,
1 teaspoon of spice.

DIRECTIONS:—Beat eggs separately; add yolks to butter and sugar; beat to a cream; add cream and two cups of the flour after it has been sifted in lightly; add soda and cream of tartar with the rest of the flour; last, add spices and beat all well; bake in jelly tins. Ice between and on top with the following icing: Whites of 2 eggs, 1½ cups of loaf sugar, and the blackberry preserves.

A SWISS ROLL.

4 eggs,
¼ lb of flour,
1 teaspoon of vanilla,
1 cup of white sugar,
¼ teaspoon of salt,

DIRECTIONS:—Beat the eggs thoroughly, first sifting the sugar in; add the flour by degrees, adding the salt to the flour; last, add the flavoring; line a flat tin with buttered paper; bake in a rather quick oven, and when done remove and spread with any good jell; roll up, and when cold slice and serve with any good sauce that is preferred.

WHITE CREAM CAKE—GOOD.

8 eggs, whites only,
2 cups of loaf sugar,
4 large cups of flour,
1½ cups of cream,
1 small cup of butter,
2 teaspoons of orange extract,
3 teaspoons of baking powder.

DIRECTIONS:—Whip the whites of the eggs stiff; cream the butter and sugar together; add one cup of the cream, then two cups of the flour sifted in; next the other half cup of cream and another cup of flour; last, sift the baking powder with the remaining cup of flour, and add this and the eggs and flavoring beat up well for five minutes; then butter some square jelly tins, and bake quick, not letting them get too much crust or too brown, as this spoils the cake.

Use the following cream filling:—2 cups of white sugar, 1½ cups cold water, ¼ teaspoon cream of tartar, 1 teaspoon orange extract, whites of 3 eggs. DIRECTIONS—Put sugar on to cook; boil until it will be creamy, by putting on the whites of the eggs, on a cool plate and beating awhile; add cream of tartar when first putting on to cook, but do not stir while boiling. After taking off of the stove add four tablespoons of thick sweet cream, and one cup of powdered loaf sugar spread between cake and on top. Flavor the last thing.

ICE CREAM CAKE.

¾ cup of butter,
2 cups of white sugar,
1 cup of sweet milk,
3 cups of flour,
1 teaspoon of vanilla,
Whites of 7 eggs,
2 teaspoons of baking powder.

Bake in jelly tins, quick and soft. Beat butter and sugar to a cream; add some flour and the milk; last add baking powder sifted in the rest of the flour; flavor with vanilla.

Directions for Icing:—One cup of boiling water poured over three cups of white sugar; boil slowly till it will string from the spoon; pour while hot over the whites of three eggs after they have been beaten; stir till it begins to cool; spread on top and between cake; flavor with same as cake.

CREAM FILLING FOR CAKES, NO. 2.

Whites of 3 eggs,
2 cups of sugar,
1 teaspoon of vanilla,
3 tablespoons of thick cream.

DIRECTIONS:—Whip the eggs lightly; add the sugar by degrees, using the powdered loaf sugar; then add the cream and flavoring last; it is better to heat the cream and let it cool before using, do not scald it as this will spoil the flavor. This filling will be found excellent. The sugar can be boiled and poured over the beaten whites; then beat till cold; proceed as above if the cakes are intended to be kept for any length of time.

COFFEE FILLING FOR CAKES.

1 cup of coffee,
1 cup of cream,
1 cup of sugar,
1 heaping teaspoon of gelatine,
2 eggs.

DIRECTIONS:—Make the coffee very strong; add the sugar; then the cream: have good rich cream, must be sweet; dissolve gelatine in a little milk over hot water, add to the other mixture; beat the eggs thoroughly and pour on the hot coffee; stir well together; put between the layers of cake when partly cooled.

CHOCOLATE FILLING.

10 tablespoons of chocolate,
3 tablespoons of corn starch,
1 large tablespoon of butter,
½ cup of sugar,
½ cup of milk.

DIRECTIONS:—Grate chocolate; add sugar; dissolve corn starch in milk; then add the butter; put on stove, cook until like a custard; remove and beat up well and it is ready to spread between the cakes.

COOKED ICING.

3 cups of granulated sugar,
Whites of 3 eggs,
1 teaspoon of lemon,
½ teaspoon of cream of tartar,
1 cup of boiling water.

DIRECTIONS—Put sugar and water together; set in boiling water, boil till ropy or stringy; have eggs beaten stiff; pour the mixture boiling hot over the eggs and beat until almost cold; flavor and add cream of tartar dissolved in a teaspoon of cold water; use immediately.

TO MAKE ICING WITHOUT COOKING.

To the white of one egg allow eight tablespoons of loaf sugar; whisk eggs stiff; then add the sugar and one tablespoon of cold water. It will be very nice and begins to harden directly when it is put on the cake. Use same flavoring that is used in cake.

A GOOD SPONGE CAKE ROLL.

1½ teacups of sugar,
1 large cup of flour,
2 small teaspoons of baking powder,
4 eggs,
1 cup of grape jelly.

DIRECTIONS:—Whisk the eggs all together till very light; add the sugar by degrees; then baking powder sifted several times; put a pinch of salt and flavoring if desired; beat till light and put in a buttered tin and bake in a quick oven. After removing from the pan, spread with the jell and roll up and serve while hot.

Loaf Cakes.

SPONGE CAKE, NO. 1.

10 eggs,
1 ℔ of sugar,
½ ℔ of flour,
¼ teaspoon of salt,
1 lemon.

DIRECTIONS:—Beat eggs together for ten minutes; then add sugar and beat five minutes; next add some flour and juice of the lemon with the remainder of the flour and grated rind of the lemon; bake immediately after mixing, as it spoils sponge cake to stand; have a moderately hot oven. If this is made according to directions, will be very light and nice.

SPONGE CAKE, NO. 2.

6 eggs,
1½ cups of loaf sugar,
1 cup of flour,
Flavor with lemon.

DIRECTIONS:—Beat yolks and sugar; next add flour after sifting several times, a little at a time; now add the whites of the eggs beaten very stiff; last lemon; beat very quick and bake in a moderate oven.

MARBLED SPONGE CAKE NO. 3.

Whites of 9 eggs,
1½ cup of loaf sugar,
2 small spoons of cream of tartar,
1 large cup of flour,
1 teaspoon of lemon.

DIRECTIONS:—Beat eggs very stiff; sift sugar and flour together several times; add the cream of tartar; then sift this into the whites of the eggs; flavor and divide the dough and color with any good fruit coloring any color desired, and drop one spot of the white to one of the colored till all is in; bake in a moderate oven; remove from the pan; when cold turn bottom of pan up while cooling and when cold or nearly so remove and ice over with icing the same color as the cake is.

SPONGE CAKE, NO. 4.

4 eggs,
¼ pound of white sugar,
1 lemon,
¼ pound of flour.

DIRECTIONS:—Separate the eggs; beat the yolks and half of the lemon juice and sugar together until very light; then add half of the beaten whites alternate with the flour until all is used; put to bake; do not stir after all is mixed; bake in a quick oven and put paper over to avoid burning.

CREAM SPONGE CAKE.

2 cups of flour,
1½ cups of white sugar,
3 eggs,
½ cup of sweet cream,
1 teaspoon cream of tartar,
½ teaspoon of soda,
1 teaspoon of lemon extract.

DIRECTIONS.—Beat eggs thoroughly; then add cream, sugar, and one cup of flour; beat all well together; next add cream of tartar, sifted in one-half cup of flour; add this to the mixture; dissolve soda in a tablespoon of warm water and stir in; last add flavoring; bake in pan not very deep; bake quick, just so as not to burn; put in a pan with a thick paper on bottom of pan.

MOTHER'S SPONGE CAKE.

2 cups of loaf sugar,
2 cups of flour,
9 eggs,
1 heaping teaspoon baking powder,
1 teaspoon of rose flavoring.

DIRECTIONS.—First sift the sugar, that it may be light; sift flour three times; sift flour, sugar and baking powder together twice; have the eggs beat thoroughly; beat them separately, as they will be lighter; add them, a little at a time, till all is in; flavor; have pans slightly buttered; bake in an oblong pan for forty-five minutes, in a slow oven.

SPONGE GINGERBREAD.

4 cups of flour,
2 tablespoons of butter,
¾ cup of molasses,
¾ cup of sugar,
½ cup of sour milk,
1 teaspoon of soda,
½ teaspoon of cinnamon.

DIRECTIONS.—Mix sugar, molasses and butter together; add the cinnamon; beat well; then the milk, with soda dissolved in it; add flour, by sifting in by degrees; bake in a shallow bread tin. Very nice.

MOLASSES SPONGE CAKE.

1 pint of molasses,
3 cups of flour,
1 cup of sweet milk,
¼ cup of butter,
2 teaspoons of soda,
6 eggs.

DIRECTIONS.—Put molasses and butter together and beat well; next add two cups of the flour; then the milk; then the soda dissolved in one tablespoon of vinegar; now the eggs beaten together, and the remainder of the flour; bake in a tin, buttered, in a slow oven.

YELLOW POUND CAKE, NO. 1—EXCELLENT.

1 cup of butter,
2 cups of white sugar,
3½ cups of flour,
½ cup of sweet milk
¼ cup of brandy,
Yolks of 6 eggs and 3 whole ones,
1½ teaspoons of soda,
2 teaspoons of cream of tartar,
¼ pound of citron,
1 cup of raisins,
1 cup of currants.

DIRECTIONS:—Beat butter, sugar and yolks of the eggs for 15 minutes; then add milk and two cups of flour; then the beaten eggs and the other cup and a half of flour, with cream of tartar sifted in it; then add the fruit dredged in flour, and citron sliced thin; last add soda dissolved in a little warm water; beat well; bake in a moderate oven.

POUND CAKE, NO. 2.

1 pound pulverized sugar,
1 pound of flour,
1 pound of butter,
9 eggs,
1 wine glass of good brandy.

DIRECTIONS:—Beat the butter to a cream; beat the eggs separately, then add the yolks and sugar to the butter and beat 15 minutes; next sift in the flour; add brandy a little at a time; after brandy is all added, beat the whites of the eggs in lightly and beat the mixture all one half an hour. Beat with upward strokes as the mixture depends largely on the lightness of it. Bake in a slow oven.

GOLDEN FRUIT CAKE, NO. 1.

1½ pounds of butter,
Yolks of 15 eggs,
1½ pounds of white sugar,
3 teaspoons of baking powder,
1 cup of molasses,
1 pound of figs,
2 pounds sweet almonds,
½ pound of citron,
½ pound of candied cherries.

DIRECTIONS.—Cream the butter and add to the sugar and yolks of the eggs; beat twenty minutes; then add molasses and some of the flour; now add the remainder of the flour, with the baking powder sifted in; blanch the almonds by putting them in hot water and removing the skins; after the outside hull has been taken off, chop fine and add to the fruit, which also must be chopped; slice the citron; dredge in flour and add to cake; bake two hours in a moderate oven.

FRUIT CAKE, NO. 1.

1 pound of brown sugar,
1 pound of butter,
10 eggs,
1 pound of flour,
1 pound each of raisins and figs,
1 pound of currants,
½ pound of candied citron,
1 nutmeg,
2 tablepoons each of spice and cinnamon,
1 tablespoon of cloves,
2 teaspoons of baking powder.

DIRECTIONS.—Beat the eggs separately; beat both butter and sugar to a cream; then add the beaten yolks; add a little of the flour at a time; now the whites, after they have been sufficiently beaten; seed raisins; chop all fruit fine in a chopping bowl; slice citron very thin and add last; dredge all thoroughly in flour; sift baking powder in some of the flour and add the last thing, after the spices; bake very slowly.

FRUIT CAKE, NO. 3. EXCELLENT.

1 pound white sugar,
1 cup of molasses,
1 cup of butter,
1 teaspoon of soda,
1¼ pounds of flour,
12 eggs,
2 pounds of raisins,
2 pounds of currants,
¼ pound of candied lemon peel,
1 wine glass of good brandy,
1½ teaspoons of spice,
1 teaspoon of cloves,
1 whole nutmeg.

DIRECTIONS:—Cream butter; add sugar and beat thoroughly; then add yolks of the eggs; then a little flour; part of the whites of the eggs well beaten; add flour and whites till all is used; chop fruit fine and dredge in flour and add also spices; add brandy last; beat thoroughly. This cake requires a very large pan and a slow oven; try with a straw to ascertain when done; it requires about three hours to bake. Dissolve soda in a little warm water and add last; mix with the hands, as the dough is most too stiff to mix with a spoon or paddle.

FRUIT CAKE, NO. 1.

1 pound of butter,
9 eggs,
½ teaspoon of soda,
1¼ pounds of flour,
1 pound of loaf sugar,
½ pound of currants,
½ pound of raisins,
¼ pounds each of citron and lemon peel,
¾ pound of sweet almonds. (no spices.)

DIRECTIONS.—Cream butter and sugar together; sift flour; beat eggs separately; add yolks first, then some flour, then whites and rest of flour; next fruit, after it has been chopped and dredged in flour; slice citron and lemon peel, dredge them in flour; last add almonds, after they have been blanched; bake in a slow oven. This will require about two hours to bake. Dissolve soda in a little warm water and add; mix well.

FRUIT CAKE, NO. 5.

1 cup of sugar,
1 cup of molasses,
1 cup of butter,
1 cup of sweet milk,
9 whole eggs,
½ pound each of raisins, figs and currants,
1 teaspoon of spice and cinnamon,
2 teaspoons of cloves,
1 teaspoon of soda.

DIRECTIONS.—Beat butter, sugar and molasses together; add eggs, beaten separately; next, alternately, the flour and milk; after this is added, dredge the fruit in flour and add, a handful at a time; then lastly the spices, sifted with a little of the flour, and soda dissolved in warm water; make batter stiff; bake as previous cakes, in a slow oven. It will require about two and one-half hours to bake.

FRUIT CAKE, NO. 6.

1 cup of brown sugar,
1½ cups of molasses,
1 cup of butter,
4 large cups of flour,
6 whole eggs,
1 cup of sweet milk,
1 lb of raisins, currants and figs together, equal parts,
1 heaping teaspoon of soda,
1 teaspoon each of all kinds of spices.

DIRECTIONS:—Cream butter and sugar; add the molasses and beaten yolks, then half the flour; then beat 20 minutes or more; then add beaten whites and the rest of the flour, fruit, and spices; beat ten minutes; add soda last, dissolved in water; bake in a very slow oven for about one and one-half hours.

PLUM CAKE.

2 pounds of white sugar,
1 pound of butter,
Yolks of 10 eggs and whites of 15,
2 pounds of sifted flour,
1 cup of sweet cream,
1 teaspoon of soda dissolved in milk,
2 teaspoons of cream of tartar sifted in flour,
½ pound of citron,
2 pounds of blanched almonds,
2 pounds of raisins and currants together,
2 tablespoons of cinnamon,
1 teaspoon of cloves,
1 tablespoon of spice,
1 nutmeg.

DIRECTIONS:—Prepare same as fruit cake; bake in a very large pan; have two thickness of paper in bottom and bake in a moderate oven for four hours; be sure that it is well done. This cake will keep for six months.

WHITE CAKE, NO. 1.

Whites of 12 eggs,
2 cups of butter,
2½ cups of sugar,
1 cup of water,
1 teaspoon of rose flavoring,
2 teaspoons of baking powder,
4 cups of flour.

DIRECTIONS:—Beat sugar and butter for ten minutes; then add a little of the water and flour, and water again to flour till all but a cup of flour is left to sift the baking powder in; now add the whites of the eggs beaten stiff; and flavoring and cup of flour; beat five minutes longer and put in a greased tin and bake in a moderate oven. In all, beat this one-half an hour.

WHITE CAKE, NO. 2.

Whites of 16 eggs,
2 small cups of butter,
3 cups of sugar,
2 cups of milk,
6 cups of flour,
3 teaspoons of baking powder,
2 teaspoons of flavoring.

DIRECTIONS:—Beat butter to a cream; add sugar, beat 15 minutes; then add a little milk and flour alternately till all but one cup is used; then add whites of the eggs and the cup of flour with the baking powder sifted in, and flavoring; do not beat but five minutes after last flour and baking powder is added; bake in a moderate oven; try with a straw and if no dough adheres to straw, the cake will do to remove from the oven.

WHITE CURRANT CAKE.

1½ pounds of flour.
1 pound of white sugar,
¾ pound of butter,
Whites of 11 eggs,
1 gill of sweet milk,
1 teaspoon of soda,
2 teaspoons cream of tartar,
1 pound of currants.

DIRECTIONS.—Put butter and sugar together and beat five minutes; add milk and flour, alternately; next add beaten whites of the eggs, and soda dissolved in about two tablespoons of water; now add cream of tartar, sifted in a little flour; last add currants, dredged in flour, after being well cleaned; bake in a slow oven for two and one-half hours.

ANGEL CAKE, NO 1

1 tumbler of flour,
1½ tumblers of sugar.
Whites of 15 eggs,
1 teaspoon of cream of tartar.
1 large teaspoon of vanilla.

DIRECTIONS.—Sift sugar three times; then add cream of tartar; put sugar and flour together, and sift three times; then put in sieve again and sift a little at a time into the beaten whites of the eggs. They must be beaten very stiff and none allowed to settle at the bottom, as that will hinder the lightness of the cake; after all is added beat lightly for ~~ten~~ 2 minutes; put in an unbuttered pan; place in the oven; do not open the door for twenty minutes; have the oven not very hot and bake one hour; put lemon or vanilla last thing. This is excellent.

GOLD AND SILVER CAKE.

GOLD PART.

Yolks of 6 eggs,
1½ cups of sugar,
½ cup of butter,
3 cups of flour,
1 cup of sweet milk,
1 teaspoon of cream of tartar,
½ teaspoon of soda,
1 teaspoon of vanilla.

DIRECTIONS:—Cream butter, sugar, and yolks of the eggs together; add half of the flour; next the milk; next the cream of tartar in remainder of flour; next the soda dissolved in a little warm water; last the vanilla; bake in jelly tins in a rather quick oven.

SILVER PART.

Whites of 6 eggs,
1½ cups of white sugar,
1 cup of butter,
3 cups of flour,
1 cup of sweet milk,
2 teaspoons cream of tartar,
1 teaspoon of soda,
1 teaspoon of lemon extract.

DIRECTIONS:—Cream butter and sugar together; add milk and flour alternately; reserve a little of flour to mix with cream of tartar; dissolve soda in a little warm water; then add the remainder of the flour and cream of tartar; next whip the whites to a stiff froth and then add the flavoring; bake in a rather quick oven. Fill between with any filling desired.

ANGEL CAKE, NO. 2.

Whites of 11 eggs,
1½ tumblers of white sugar,
1 tumbler of flour,
1 teaspoon of cream of tartar,
1 teaspoon of vanilla.

DIRECTIONS:—Mix same as number one, but do not bake but forty minutes. Angel cake should never be removed until they are entirely cold; turn pan upside down on a plate to cool.

CITRON CAKE.

1 quart of flour,
1 cup of butter,
2 cups of white sugar,
12 eggs,
1 cup of cream,
½ pound of citron,
1 teaspoon extract of sweet almond,
2 teaspoons of baking powder.

DIRECTIONS.—Cream butter and sugar, after it has been sifted; then add yolks of the eggs; beat well; then add the cream and some of the flour sifted in; add next, the whites, beaten very stiff, next the citron, sliced thin and dredged in flour; last flavoring; bake in a moderate oven.

LOAF CAKE.

1 cup of butter,
2 cup of white sugar,
1 cup of milk,
3 cups of flour,
Whites of 11 eggs.
1 teaspoon of baking powder,
1 teaspoon of vanilla,

DIRECTIONS.—Beat butter to a cream; sift sugar three times and add, a little at a time; beat the butter till creamy; add milk, and flour, that has been sifted four times, with baking powder in it; beat well and add the whites, after they have been beaten stiff, a little at a time, and the last cup of flour; put the cake in tin and bake three-fourths of an hour, in a moderate oven. When made properly, this is almost like angel food, and is very nice.

DATE CAKE.

1 cup brown sugar,
1 cup of molasses,
1 small cup of butter,
1 cup of sweet cider,
4 eggs,
1 teaspoon of soda,
4 cups of flour,
1 cup of dates.

DIRECTIONS:—Mix butter, sugar and yolks of the eggs together; next add the cider and half of the flour; now beat the whites of the eggs well; add to mixture; put soda in a little warm water, stir in and add the rest of the flour and dates stoned and dredged in flour; put in an oblong pan and bake till well done in a moderate oven. This makes a cake that is almost equal to fruit cake and will keep almost as well.

FEATHER CAKE.

Whites of three eggs,
1 cup of white sugar,
¼ cup of butter,
½ cup of sweet milk,
3 cups of flour,
2 teaspoons of baking powder,
1 teaspoon of sweet almonds.

DIRECTIONS:—Cream butter and sugar together; add the milk and two cups of flour; beat the whites of the eggs very stiff and add them; now sift baking powder with remaining cup of flour and sift it three times in flour; last the flavoring; bake in a moderate oven. This, if properly made, is very nice.

TEA CAKE.

2 cups of sugar,
½ cup of butter,
3 eggs,
½ cup of sweet cream,
3 cups of flour,
½ teaspoon of soda,
1 teaspoon cream of tartar,
¼ teaspoon of nutmeg.

DIRECTIONS.—Sift sugar twice; add this to butter, and whip till light; beat eggs separately; add the yolks to the butter and sugar; now sift the flour, with the cream of tartar in it; add the cream first; then sift the flour in lightly, and beaten whites of the eggs; dissolve soda in a little warm water; add lastly, the nutmeg, grated; bake in a moderate oven.

PUFF CAKE.

1 cup of white sugar,
¼ cup of butter,
4 tablespoons of cream,
2 eggs,
1 teaspoon of cream of tartar,
½ teaspoon of soda,
2 cups of flour,
1 teaspoon of lemon.

DIRECTIONS.—Beat butter, sugar, eggs and cream till light and foamy; then add the flour, a little at a time, with the cream of tartar sifted twice into it; last add the soda, dissolved in a little warm water, and after this, flavor and beat a few minutes longer. You will find this cake very light and suitable to eat with fruit or cream. Bake in a shallow pan.

AMERICAN FLAG CAKE.

RED PART.

2½ cups of flour,
1 cup of red sugar,
½ cup of butter,
¾ cup of sweet milk,
Whites of 5 eggs,
1 heaping teaspoon of baking powder,
Flavor with strawberry.

DIRECTIONS:—Cream butter; add sugar after it has been rolled and sifted; beat eggs stiff; add flour and eggs alternately; have the baking powder well sifted into the flour; add the milk and lastly the flavoring.

WHITE PART.

1 cup of loaf sugar,
½ cup of butter,
¾ cup of sweet milk,
Whites of 5 eggs,
2½ cups of flour,
1 heaping teaspoon of baking powder,
Flavor with lemon.

DIRECTIONS:—Beat sugar and butter well together; add milk and two cups of flour; beat eggs and add them; next one half cup of flour with baking powder sifted in; add the flavoring; beat well.

BLUE PART.

1 cup of blue sugar,
¾ cup of sweet milk,
½ cup of butter,
Whites of 5 eggs,
2½ cups of flour,
1 teaspoon of baking powder,
Vanilla flavoring.

DIRECTIONS:—Sift sugar well; add butter and beat together; then add milk and flour alternately till two cups of flour is used; sift the baking powder in one-half cup of flour; add the beaten whites and flavoring; beat all well together.

After all is ready, take a good sized pan and first put in the red dough, then the white and blue on top; have a moderate oven and try with a straw to see when it is sufficiently done; remove from pan and let cool and ice with three colors in circles. This is a handsome cake and suitable for the Fourth of July.

ECONOMICAL CAKE.

4 eggs,
1½ cups of sugar,
2 oz. of butter,
1 cup of cold water,
3 cups of flour,
1 large teaspoon of baking powder.

DIRECTIONS:—Beat yolks of eggs with sugar and butter till very light; add water and one half of the flour; beat smooth; add the whites beaten smoothly and the other half of the flour with the baking powder; flavor with nutmeg; mix well and bake in a moderate oven.

ENGLISH CAKE.

1 pound of butter,
1 pound of white sugar,
1 pint of sweet milk,
2 pounds of flour,
1 teacup of good yeast sponge,
½ pound of raisins,
½ pound of currants,
1 teaspoon of nutmeg,
¼ pound of candied citron,

DIRECTIONS:—Cream butter and sugar together and set aside till needed; heat the milk slightly, then stir in the flour and add a pinch of salt and the cup of sponge; set to rise; when light, then add the sugar and butter and a little more flour, about a cupful if needed, as sometimes it will seem sticky and dough thin; beat well; dredge fruit in flour; after citron has been sliced and currants washed and dried and raisins stemmed and chopped, add and mix well; add nutmeg; put in pan and let rise and bake in a moderate oven.

SOFT GINGER BREAD, NO. 2.

½ cup of fresh butter,
1 cup of molasses,
1 teaspoon of ginger,
1 teaspoon of soda,
½ cup of hot water,
½ teaspoon of salt,

DIRECTIONS:—Put lard and molasses together; add water with soda dissolved in it; now stir flour in; add the ginger last; put flour in till moderately stiff, but not too much so, as that would spoil the lightness of the cakes; bake in a hot oven, not hot enough to burn. This is very nice when properly made.

SOFT GINGER BREAD, NO. 1.

1 cup of molasses,
½ cup of brown sugar,
½ cup of butter,
1 cup of boiling water,
3 eggs,
1½ pints of flour,
1 teaspoon of ginger,
½ cup of sour cream,
1 teaspoon of soda.

DIRECTIONS.—Beat butter and sugar together; add molasses and the beaten eggs; beat them together, and add hot water, with soda dissolved in it; have the teaspoon heaping, both of soda and ginger; add milk and ginger; now stir in the flour and beat well for a few minutes and put in a greased tin; bake in a moderate oven.

CHOCOLATE CAKE, NO. 1.

1½ cup of sugar,
½ cups of butter,
4 eggs,
½ cup of milk,
2 cups of flour,
1 teaspoon of baking powder,
½ cake of chocolate,
1 teaspoon of vanilla.

DIRECTIONS.—Beat the yolks of the eggs well, and add butter and sugar; beat till it is very light; then add the milk, and one cup of the flour; grate the chocolate in; now add the beaten whites and the other cup of flour, with the baking powder; last flavoring: bake in a medium size pan, in a moderate oven.

CHOCOLATE LOAF CAKE, NO 2.

½ cup of butter,
1 cup of milk,
1½ cups of white sugar,
3 cups of flour,
½ cup of coffee,
2 teaspoons of baking powder,
5 eggs,
2 teaspoons of vanilla,
2 tablespoons of chocolate.

DIRECTIONS:—Beat butter, sugar, and yolks of the eggs to a cream; next add one cup of the flour and after this the milk; now grate the chocolate in the hot coffee; this must be hot; next add another cup of flour and the beaten whites of the eggs; now put baking powder in the third cup of flour; sift three times and add to the mixture; last the vanilla; bake in a moderate oven.

PICNIC CAKE.

½ cup of butter,
2 small cups of sugar,
1 cup of cream,
4 cups of flour,
2 teaspoons of baking powder,
6 eggs,
1 teacup of raisins,
1 teaspoon of lemon,

DIRECTIONS:—Beat butter, sugar and yolks of the eggs together; add the cream and three cups of flour; next the whites of the eggs beaten well; now add the fourth cup of flour, with the baking powder; add the lemon; last the raisins dredged in flour; bake in a moderate oven.

PORK CAKE, NO. 1.

1 pound of currants,
1 pound of raisins,
4 cups of flour,
1 pound of pork fat,
1 cup of molasses,
1 cup of brown sugar,
1 cup of boiling water,
2 teaspoons of soda,
½ teaspoon of cloves,
1 teaspoon of cinnamon,
1 teaspoon of spices,
1 teaspoon of salt.

DIRECTIONS.—Chop the pork; add molasses and boiling water, with the soda dissolved in it; now sift the flour and stir in; have currants cleaned and dry, and raisins chopped fine; dredge both in flour; add spices and salt; beat well and put in an oblong pan and bake in a slow oven. It will take about two hours to bake.

PORK CAKE, NO. 2.

1¼ pounds of pork fat,
1 pint of hot coffee,
1½ cups of molasses,
1 cup of brown sugar,
1 teaspoon each of all kinds of spices,
1½ pounds of currants,
1 pound of raisins.
½ pound of figs.
¼ pound of citron,
2 teaspoons of soda.

DIRECTIONS.—Chop pork fine in bowl; pour coffee over this; next add molasses, with soda dissolved in them; now add sugar and flour enough to make a stiff batter; dredge the fruit, after carefully preparing it; slice citron; dredge also with the fruit; add spices last. Do not put pepper or ginger in this cake. Bake about two or two and one-half hours in a moderate oven.

WATERMELON CAKE.

WHITE PART.

1 cup of white sugar,
¼ cup of butter,
½ cup of milk,
Whites of 6 eggs,
3 cups of flour,
2 teaspoons of baking powder,
1 teaspoon of strawberry flavoring,

RED PART.

1 cup of red sugar,
¼ cup of butter,
½ cup of milk,
Whites of 4 eggs,
2½ cups of flour,
2 teaspoons of baking powder,
1 cup of raisins.

Directions for white part:—Cream butter and sugar; add the milk and 2 cups of flour, whites of the eggs beaten well; add third cup of flour, with the baking powder sifted in; last add flavoring.

Directions for red part:—Beat butter and sifted sugar together; add milk; next half the flour and baking powder sifted in some of the flour; put white part around the edge of the pan; next put some of the red part without the raisins; then some with the raisins to represent the seeds of the melon; bake in a moderate oven. This is a very beautiful cake.

COFFEE CAKE.

1 cup of butter,
2 cups of brown sugar,
1 cup of coffee,
4 cups of flour,
2 teaspoons of baking powder,
Yolks of 7 eggs,
½ teaspoon of cloves,
1 teaspoon of cinnamon,
1 teaspoon of nutmeg,
1 teaspoon of spice,
1 cup of raisins,
¼ cup of citron,
½ cup of hickory nut meats.

DIRECTIONS:—Cream butter and sugar together; whip yolks of eggs and add; sift the flour and add a little; then some of the cold coffee; the coffee must be strong; then add a little flour till half is used; the other half must have baking powder sifted into it; dredge the fruit and add nuts and spices; beat twenty minutes; bake in moderate oven.

GINGER BREAD.

5 cups of flour,
1½ cups of brown sugar,
1½ cups of molasses,
1 cup sour cream,
4 eggs,
½ cup of butter,
1 tablespoon of ginger,
2 teaspoons of soda.

DIRECTIONS:—Beat eggs together till very light; add butter and sugar and molasses; beat well; sift in some of the flour; now add the cream with the soda well dissolved in it; add the remainder of the flour and ginger; bake in shallow tins in a rather moderate oven. This is a good recipe for making ginger bread.

CUP CAKE.

1 cup of butter,
2 cups of sugar,
4 eggs,
1 cup of milk,
3 cups of flour,
2 teaspoons of baking powder,
1 lemon.

DIRECTIONS:—Beat butter and sugar to a cream; add the beaten yolks and milk and flour with the powder sifted in, then the beaten whites, and juice and the grated rind of the lemon; beat thoroughly and put in a tin and it will take about one hour to bake in a moderate oven.

MARBLE CAKE.

LIGHT PART.

Whites of 7 eggs,
2 cups of loaf sugar,
1 large cup of butter,
1 cup of sweet milk,
4 cups of flour,
2 teaspoons of baking powder,
1 teaspoon of lemon or vanilla.

DARK PART.

Yolks of 7 eggs,
1 cup of brown sugar,
1 cup of molasses,
1 cup of butter,
4 cups of flour,
1 cup of sweet milk,
2 teaspoons of baking powder,
1 teaspoon of cinnamon,
½ teaspoon of cloves,
1 teaspoon of spice,
½ teaspoon of soda,
1 teaspoon of nutmeg.

Directions for light part:—Cream butter and sugar; next add two cups of flour, and the remainder of the flour and baking powder, and whites of the eggs beaten very stiff; last add the flavoring.

Directions for dark part:—Beat butter and sugar to a cream; add yolks and beat thoroughly; add the molasses with the soda dissolved in it; then the milk and two cups of flour, and the remainder with the baking powder sifted in; last the spices. Bake in a moderate oven till well done.

BLACK CAKE.

1 pound of currants,
1 pound of raisins,
½ pound of citron,
1 pound of almonds,
16 eggs,
1 pound of brown sugar,
1 pound of flour,
1 pound of butter,
1 tablespoon of spice,
1 tablespoon of cinnamon,
1 teaspoon of cloves,
1 wine glass of brandy,
1 heaping teaspoon of soda,
2 heaping teaspoons of cream of tartar,

DIRECTIONS:—Cream the butter and sugar together; then add the yolks and flour, a little at a time, alternately, with the beaten whites of the eggs; next add brandy, and soda dissolved in one tablespoon of hot water; now the rest of the flour sifted in; next spices; slice the citron, stone the raisins, if no seedless raisins can be secured; clean currants and dry, and dredge in flour; blanch the almonds by putting in hot water a few minutes and removing skins, having hull off before putting in hot water; dry on a cloth and pound or chop them and add to fruit; dredge also in flour. Bake in a slow oven till well done.

BERRY CAKE.

2 cups of flour,
1 cup of milk,
1 cup of sugar,
Whites of 4 eggs, yolks of 2,
½ cup of butter,
1 pint of berries,
2 small teaspoons of baking powder.

DIRECTIONS:—Beat the whites of the four eggs and yolks of the two together, and then add sugar, butter and beat thoroughly; add milk and one-half of the flour; sift the baking powder with the remainder of the flour; if the berries are damp dry them in the sun or in a dry cloth; dredge lightly in flour; then add to the cake. This is good for blackberry, or any berry that is preferred. Bake in a slow oven.

COOKIES.

GINGER COOKIES.

½ cup of sugar,
1 cup of molasses,
1 cup of butter,
1 egg,
1 teaspoon of vinegar,
1 tablespoon of ginger,
1 teaspoon of soda dissolved in hot water.

DIRECTIONS:—Mix like cooky dough, rather soft, and bake in a moderate oven.

GINGER SNAPS.

1 cup of molasses,
1 cup brown sugar,
⅔ cup of lard,
1 teaspoon of ground ginger,
1 teaspoon of soda,
½ teaspoon of salt.

DIRECTIONS:—Mix all these together; put in a tin pan and boil until it thickens a little; now stir in by degrees one cup of flour; after it is well heated, add the soda dissolved in a little warm water; mix well before taking from the stove; add flour enough to make a stiff dough; roll out thin; bake in a quick oven.

HARD GINGER BREAD.

2 cups of molasses,
1 cup of sugar,
1 cup of butter,
1 heaping teaspoon of ginger,
2 teaspoons of soda,
1 cup of sour cream.

DIRECTIONS:—Cream the butter with the sugar; add molasses; then soda dissolved in sour cream; add ginger, and take a mixing bowl and put enough flour to make stiff enough to roll out and cut in squares, and bake a golden brown in a moderate oven.

HICKORY NUT COOKIES.

1 cup of sugar,
2 eggs,
½ cup of melted butter,
6 tablespoons of milk,
1 teaspoon of cream of tartar,
½ teaspoon of soda,
1 cup of chopped meats.

DIRECTIONS:—Beat the eggs and butter together; add milk, and sift cream of tartar with one cup of flour; dissolve soda in a little hot water; mix all together and add the chopped meats and enough flour with the one cup of flour to make a stiff dough; roll out thin; cut with a cake cutter and bake in a quick oven.

GRAHAM COOKIES.

½ cup of sour cream, (thick)
1 cup of sugar,
½ teaspoon of soda.

DIRECTIONS.—Mix with graham flour to roll out; bake in an oven not as hot as for white flour cookies, as it takes longer to bake them.

COCOANUT COOKIES.

1½ cups of sugar,
1 cup of butter,
2 eggs,
1 teaspoon of soda,
½ cup of sour cream,
1 cup of cocoanut.

DIRECTIONS.—Roll and sift the sugar; cream the butter and add; beat the eggs till light and add to the sugar and butter, then dissolve the soda in the sour cream; add the cup of grated cocoanut; mix well together with enough flour to roll out nicely, but not too stiff; roll out thin and sprinkle with sugar and bake a nice brown.

DOUGHNUTS, NO. 3.

1 cup of sour cream,
1½ cups of sugar,
1 cup of butter,
3 eggs,
1 teaspoon of lemon,
1 teaspoon of cream of tartar,
½ teaspoon of soda.

DIRECTIONS.—Mix butter, sugar and eggs together; add cream, with soda dissolved in it; add lemon; make stiff enough to roll out and cut with doughnut cutter; fry in one-third butter and two-thirds lard; after taking out roll in cinnamon then in sugar.

CREAM DOUGHNUTS, NO. 2.

1 cup of thick sweet cream,
1 cup of white sugar,
2 eggs,
½ teaspoon of soda,
1 teaspoon of cream of tartar,
¼ teaspoon of nutmeg.

DIRECTIONS:—Mix cream and sugar; add the eggs after being beaten light; next add cream with soda dissolved in it; sift cream of tartar in the flour; add enough to make a stiff dough, roll out and cut in strips; roll around a stick and fry in hot grease to a light brown.

DOUGHNUTS, NO. 1.

1 cup of sugar,
½ cup of thick sour cream,
1 teaspoon of soda,
¼ teaspoon of nutmeg,
1 egg.

DIRECTIONS:—Put sugar and egg together; beat well; next add cream with soda dissolved in it; add nutmeg; use enough flour to make a stiff dough; roll out and cut with a doughnut cutter and fry in fresh lard a golden brown; have lard smoking hot, but do not let it scorch.

CRULLERS.

¼ cup of butter,
2 eggs,
1 cup of sugar,
1 cup of sour milk,
1 teaspoon of soda.

DIRECTIONS:—Mix butter, sugar and eggs together; dissolve soda in milk and add this to the flour and make a stiff dough; roll out one fourth inch in thickness, cut and fry in hot lard; take out and roll in white sugar.

WAFERS.

1 cup of flour,
¼ cup of sugar
¼ cup of cream,
1 tablespoon of butter,
¼ teaspoon of mace,
¼ teaspoon of orange peel,
1 egg,
¼ teaspoon of soda.

DIRECTIONS.—Sift flour; beat sugar and egg together; then add the butter; beat five minutes before adding the cream, orange and mace; grate the orange peel; sift the flour in; add the soda, dissolved in warm water. The cream must be sweet; bake in wafer irons. To be eaten with any good jam and cream.

COOKIES, NO. 3.

2 cups of sugar,
1 cup of butter,
2 eggs,
4 tablespoons of sour cream,
1 teaspoon of caraway seeds,
1 teaspoon of soda.

DIRECTIONS.—Cream the sugar and butter; beat the eggs and add to the sugar and butter; dissolve soda in the cream; add all this to flour enough to roll stiff; add the caraway seed last; work well; roll out, and cut in shapes; bake in a moderate oven.

SUGAR COOKIES, NO. 1.

2 eggs,
1 cup of sugar,
1 cup of butter,
1 teaspoon of nutmeg,
1 teaspoon of soda,
½ cup of sour cream.

DIRECTIONS:—Mix stiff; roll out very thin; sprinkle with sugar and bake in a moderately quick oven.

SUGAR COOKIES, NO. 2.

½ cup of butter,
1 cup of sugar,
1 egg,
¼ teaspoon of soda,
½ cup of sweet milk,

DIRECTIONS:—Cream butter, sugar and eggs together; add soda dissolved in milk; mix stiff with flour and cut out and bake in a quick oven.

BOSTON COOKIES.

1 cup of butter,
1½ cups of sugar,
2 cups of flour,
1 cup of raisins chopped fine,
½ teaspoon of soda dissolved in warm water,
3 eggs,
Flavor to suit taste.

DIRECTIONS:—Mix well; roll thin; cut into shapes and put into the pans; have dough rather stiff, and sprinkle granulated sugar over each.

JUMBLES, NO. 2.

½ pound of butter,
3 eggs,
½ pound of sugar,
¾ pound of flour,
2 teaspoons of rose water.

DIRECTIONS:—Beat the butter and sugar to a cream; add eggs well beaten; then rose water; then the flour; dust the molding board with flour; roll out the mixture about one-eighth of an inch thick; cut with a doughnut cutter, thus forming rings; bake in a moderate oven until a light brown; dust sugar over after removing from oven.

JUMBLES, NO. 3.

½ pound of butter,
9 oz. of flour,
½ pound of powdered sugar,
1 teaspoon of vanilla,
2 wine glasses of brandy,
4 eggs.

DIRECTIONS:—Beat the butter to a cream; add the sugar gradually, beating until very light; now beat the eggs all together; add to the butter and sugar; add brandy and vanilla, and last the flour sifted in; beat all well together; drop by spoonfuls on buttered paper; bake in a moderate oven until the edges are a delicate brown.

JUMBLES, NO. 1.

1 pint of sweet cream,
3 eggs,
2 teaspoons of baking powder,
2 cups of sugar,
½ teaspoon of salt,
1 quart of flour,
1 teaspoon of cinnamon.

DIRECTIONS.—Sift the two teaspoons of baking powder, sugar and salt into the flour; add the eggs, cinnamon and cream; make into a stiff dough; roll rather thin; fry in hot lard till a nice brown.

SCOTCH CAKES.

½ pound of flour,
½ pound of butter,
½ pound of sugar,
2 eggs,
1 teaspoon cinnamon.

DIRECTIONS.—Mix flour, sugar, butter and eggs well together; add cinnamon, and mix; roll out into a thin sheet; cut with a cutter; bake in a moderate oven till well done.

GINGER COOKIES.

1 cup of molasses,
1 cup of brown sugar,
1 cup of butter,
1 cup of warm water,
1 teaspoon of ginger,
1½ teaspoon of soda.

DIRECTIONS.—Mix all the ingredients together; then add enough flour to make a rather stiff dough; roll out and cut with a cake cutter; bake in a slow oven, as any cake that has molasses is easily burned. Be sure and dissolve the soda in the water and add to the rest of the mixture.

ORANGE CAKES.

½ pint sweet milk,
1 pound of sugar,
½ teaspoon of lemon juice,
½ pound of butter,
¼ teaspoon of soda,
3 eggs,
1 orange.

DIRECTIONS:—Beat butter and sugar together; add milk and soda dissolved in the milk; eggs beaten stiff; now sift the flour well and have enough to make a stiff dough; put all the mixture in, and the juice and grated rind of the orange; mix rather stiff; roll out and cut in small cakes and bake in a pan on a buttered paper, a nice brown; sift sugar over the dough before cutting out.

LEMON SNAPS.

1 cup of sugar,
1 cup of butter,
2 eggs,
1 teaspoon of lemon,
1 teaspoon of soda,
¼ cup of hot water.

DIRECTIONS:—Cream the butter and sugar; add the eggs after they have been whipped light; now soda dissolved in the hot water; last the lemon extract; make a stiff dough, but not as stiff as for ginger-cookies, as any cake that has molasses requires more flour; roll out thin and bake in a quick oven.

FANCY DISHES.

ALMOND MERINGUE DROPS.

7 eggs,
¾ pound of white sugar,
½ pound of blanched almonds,
1 teaspoon of rose water.

DIRECTIONS:—Blanch the almonds; try dropping them in hot water a few moments, then the inner hull will come off readily; put in a chopping bowl, chop fine; then pound to a morter; add the whites only of the eggs beaten stiff; add flavor and sugar; drop on buttered paper; bake in a moderate oven until a delicate brown.

MILLIE'S MOLASSES DROPS.

1 cup of molasses.
¼ cup of sugar,
1 cup of sour milk,
½ cup of butter,
1 teaspoon of soda.

DIRECTIONS.—Mix molasses, sugar and butter together; then flour by degrees till almost stiff enough; now dissolve soda in a little warm water and stir in; add flour till it will drop from the spoon, on buttered paper, and not run together; bake in a rather quick oven.

COCOANUT DROPS.

½ pound of cocoanut,
½ pound of white sugar,
Whites of six eggs.

DIRECTIONS.—Grate cocoanut; sift sugar; beat the eggs stiff, and mix all together; bake in a pan on buttered paper, one spoonful in a place, about one inch apart; sprinkle with sugar after removing from the oven.

ALMOND MACAROONS.

5 eggs, (whites)
2 cups of sugar,
1 pound of sweet almonds,

DIRECTIONS:—Blanch and pound almonds fine; beat whites of the eggs light and add sugar; mix well; drop on buttered paper; bake quickly; flavor with any kind of flavoring.

WHITE SPONGE FINGERS.

½ cup of flour,
1 cup of sugar,
½ teaspoon of baking powder,
Whites of 5 eggs.

DIRECTIONS:—Sift flour four times with baking powder in it; beat whites of eggs to a stiff froth; beat sugar into the whites; add next the flour and bake ten to twelve minutes in a moderate oven; when cool frost lightly with cream frosting; sprinkle with dessicated cocoanut.

COCOANUT MACAROONS.

Whites of 6 eggs,
½ pound of grated cocoanut,
1 cup of sugar.

DIRECTIONS.—Beat whites of eggs till light; then add sugar and cocoanut; drop on buttered paper by spoonfuls; bake in a moderately hot oven.

CHOCOLATE CAKES.

Whites of 6 eggs,
½ pound of grated chocolate,
1½ cups of sugar,
2 cups of sifted flour.

DIRECTIONS.—Beat the whites stiff; stir in the sugar, chocolate and flour; drop on buttered paper and bake in a quick oven.

LADY FINGERS.

8 eggs,
¾ pound of loaf sugar,
1 pound of flour,
2 small teaspoons of baking powder.

DIRECTIONS.—Beat the eggs separately; whisk the yolks light; add to the sugar; beat at least five minutes; then add the whites and flour lightly after adding the baking powder; do not stir after adding the flour, only enough to mix well; bake in a pan about an inch deep, and when perfectly cold, cut with a sharp knife, about four or five inches long by one inch wide. Very nice to line molds. For any kind of cream.

CALLA LILLIES.

Whites of 6 eggs,
1 cup of sugar,
1 cup of flour.

DIRECTIONS:—Sift sugar and flour four times; add the whites of the eggs beaten well; sift flour and sugar in lightly; flavor with strawberry; bake in a large pan so the cake will be about an inch thick; when done cut in squares; roll up in shape of a calla lily; put in small glasses and fill with whipped cream flavored with strawberry; take a piece of yellow sponge cake and cut in strips and place in the centre to represent a spadix.

LEMON CHEESE CAKE.

¼ pound of butter,
¾ pound of sugar,
5 eggs,
2 lemons.

DIRECTIONS:—Beat butter and sugar together; add eggs, except the whites of two; juice and grated rind of the lemons; put in a granite sauce pan; cook until the consistency of honey; remove to jars and it is ready for use any time. When ready to use make a good puff paste; roll out and put in patty pans, and fill with the filling and bake in a moderate oven.

DESSERT CAKE.

3 tablespoons of loaf sugar,
3 tablespoons of flour,
2 tablespoons of milk,
1 teaspoon of lemon extract,
4 eggs,
½ teaspoon of soda.

DIRECTIONS.—Sift sugar and flour; whip the yolks and sugar together; add the milk; then the beaten whites of the eggs, flour and lemon; last add the soda dissolved in a little warm water; mix lightly and put on buttered tins and bake in a quick oven.

ICE CREAM CAKES

Whites of 3 eggs,
1 small cup of white sugar,
1 large coffee cup of flour,
1 teaspoon of cream of tartar,
½ teaspoon of soda,
½ teaspoon of lemon extract,
2 tablespoons of cold water.

DIRECTIONS.—Beat eggs to a stiff froth; sift sugar and flour; sift the sugar in lightly; add the water; then the flour with the cream of tartar and soda sifted into it; flavor and drop in buttered tins, about two inches apart; bake in a quick oven; remove from oven and ice on top. Very nice with cream.

RAISIN SPIRALS.

½ cup of butter,
1 cup of sugar,
Whites of 3 eggs, yolk of 1,
½ cup of water,
1 cup of raisins,
3 cups of flour,
2 teaspoons of baking powder.

DIRECTIONS.—Cream the butter and sugar; beat the eggs very light; sift flour and baking powder together; add water to butter, sugar and eggs; put flour in a mixing bowl; chop raisins and add them; after all is mixed with the flour make stiff and roll out, and have a round stick three-fourths inche in diameter: roll around this to make a curl, and then fry in nice fresh lard, or lard and butter together; fry a nice brown and take out and roll in cinnamon, then sugar.

ORANGE BISCUITS.

Take medium sized oranges, boil them; changing the water several times; when done or tender remove them and halve, and take out the pulp and juice; then dry the peel; pound it in a mortar, till it is powdered; then measure, and take as much loaf sugar as you have of the orange powder, sift both sugar and powder of the oranges together; add the juice of the oranges; make a paste; spread rather thin on dishes and dry in the sun or before the fire, when half dry make into biscuit shape and put in the sun again till perfectly dry; then put away in boxes with white paper between. These are very nice, though requiring patience to make them.

TO MAKE SUGAR DROPS.

3 tablespoons of butter,
2 eggs,
1 large cup of flour,
½ cup of loaf sugar,
¼ teaspoon of nutmeg.

DIRECTIONS:—Whip the eggs light; add the butter and sugar; next sift the flour in and add the nutmeg; mix lightly; butter a tin and drop by spoonfuls on and put in the centre of each a candied plum; bake in a quick oven. They are very nice.

MISCELLANEOUS FOR THE TABLE.

PEACH MERINGUE.

½ dozen very ripe peaches,
6 tablespoons of sugar,
6 eggs.

DIRECTIONS.—Pare and mash the peaches; put them in a baking dish; sprinkle three tablespoons of sugar over them; whip the whites of the eggs and add the remainder of the sugar; pour over the peaches and set in the oven and brown slightly. Serve with a sauce.

A NICE APPLE DESSERT.

10 apples,
1 pound of sugar,
1 pint of water,
2 oranges,
1 pint of cream.

DIRECTIONS.—Pare the apples; cut round ways in slices about one-half inch thick; put on in a kettle; add sugar and water, having water hot; cook for five minutes; then add the apples, cook until done and clear, but do not stir or cover over; remove to a dish and add the juice of the oranges to the syrup and pour over; whip one pint of cream and sweeten; flavor with orange; when whipped very stiff, pile on top of apples in the dish. This makes a delicious dessert, as well as beautiful.

A DELICIOUS DESSERT.

1 quart of very ripe berries,
½ gallon of ice cream,

DIRECTIONS:—Pick and wash any kind of ripe berries, after draining through a colander; have the cream froen a nd put in a mold; line the mold first with the cream; then fill in with the berries and put more cream on top; pack in ice for half an hour; turn out in glass dish and serve with any good cake.

BERRY FLOAT.

Take raspberres or strawberries; sprinkle sugar over them; let stand awhile, then press through a colander to remove the seeds; to every cup of the juice and pulp add one large cup of sugar and the whites of two eggs; mix well and beat up till it will stand up in a dish. This is very nice and with the addition of a little whipped cream, is better.

BLANC MANGE.

1 quart of new milk,
5 tablespoons of corn starch,
4 tablespoons of sugar,

DIRECTIONS:—Put milk on to scald; wet the corn starch with a little of the milk before it gets warm; then add the sugar; mix well; then stir into boiling milk; cook till it thickens, then remove and put in molds that have been standing in water; when cool turn out on plates and serve with any good jelly around it, and sweet cream.

FLOAT.

1 pint of cream,
1 pint of new milk,
1 cup of sugar,
4 teaspoons of lemon,
5 eggs,
1 teaspoon of brandy.

DIRECTIONS.—Put the milk on in a double boiler; heat till scalding hot; then add the yolks of the eggs whipped light, with the sugar and a little cold milk; add to the milk and cook till it begins to thicken a little; then remove from stove and have the whites of the eggs beaten stiff; cook for a few minutes in hot water, by dropping by spoonfuls; put float in glasses and add brandy and one spoonful of the cooked whites to every glass.

GOOSEBERRY FLOAT.

1 pint of gooseberries,
1 cup of hot water,
1 tablespoon of butter,
1 cup of sugar,
2 eggs.

DIRECTIONS.—Stem and wash the berries; put on to cook in the cup of water; cook till very tender; press through a colander; add the sugar, butter and beaten yolks of the eggs; beat till it is light; put it in a glass dish; for the top, whisk the whites of the eggs very stiff; add the half cup of sugar; flavor with lemon; heap on top of the berries and serve.

BLACKBERRY MUSH.

1 quart of fresh berries,
1½ cups of sugar,
½ cup of flour,
½ pint of water.

DIRECTIONS:—Pick the berries over; pour in a kettle; add the sugar and water; when boiling add flour dissolved in a little cold water; let cook until it thickens; remove and mold. Serve with cream.

CHERRY CHEESE.

Use only very ripe red cherries; stone them; put in a bowl; wash thoroughly; to each cup of the fruit, add one cup of loaf sugar; put on to cook; simmer until it is a thick mass and will jell; keep it in tumblers; it will be very nice sliced and laid on a flat glass dish, and served with whipped cream.

A NICE WAY TO SERVE ORANGES WITH WHIPPED CREAM.

Slice them moderately thin and put one fourth of a box of gelatine to soak in cold water fifteen minutes; then pour one pint of hot water over it and one-fourth of a cup of sugar; let it set till almost cool; then have the oranges put in sauce dishes; pour the jell in each dish and when it is set, pile the whipped cream on top and set on ice until ready to serve.

SPONGE OF PINE APPLE.

1 pine apple,
1½ cups of white sugar,
1 small package of gel tine,
1½ cups of cold water,
5 eggs, (whites only)

DIRECTIONS.—Soak the gelatine two hour in one-half cup of water; chop the pineapple very fine; put into a sauce pan and cook till tender enough to press through a colander; then add gelatine, after straining it, and mix well together; remove from the stove; let it partly cool; then add the whites of the eggs, beaten stiff; whip until it begins to thicken; pour into a mold and set in a cool place or on ice. Serve with any good sauce that is preferred.

CHARLOTTE RUSSE.

¼ pound vanilla chocolate,
4 ounces of white sugar,
½ pint of new milk,
½ ounce of gelatine,
⅓ pint of whipped cream.

DIRECTIONS.—Line a mold with sponge cake; cut in slices about one inch wide; grate the chocolate in the milk; add the sugar; let boil; then dissolve the gelatine in a little milk; add the whipped cream and mix it well together: pour this over the cake in the mold till set, and then serve.

PEACH CHEESE.

6 peaches,
1 cup of white sugar,
3 eggs.

DIRECTIONS:—Pare very ripe peaches; rub through a colander; then add the sugar and yolks of the eggs beaten light; last add the whites beaten stiff; put into a buttered dish; set in the oven and bake for about fifteen minutes; serve at once with a sauce.

RICE SNOW BALLS

1 teacup of rice,
1 quart of milk,
1 pinch of salt.

DIRECTIONS:—Wash rice; put on in the cold milk, let cook till well done, but slowly as the milk is apt to burn; when done turn out in small teacups; let set and remove to a platter; serve with the following custard:

1 pint of cream,
2 eggs,
1 small cup of sugar,
1 teaspoon of flavoring.

Heat the cream; then stir the eggs in after being beaten well; cook until it thickens; then flavor and add the sugar last; let cool and pour around the snow balls.

RASPBERRY CHARLOTTE.

1 dozen lady fingers,
1 pint of cream,
½ cup of sugar,
¼ cup of raspberry juice,
1 pint of ripe berries.

DIRECTIONS:—First line a mold with lady fingers; whip the cream with sugar and raspberry juice; set on ice until almost frozen, then pour in the mold with the lady fingers; pile the cream up in the centre and put the ripe berries around on top; set on ice again; when ready to serve, remove from the mold and pour cream around it in the dish.

A VERY NICE DESSERT.

2 cups of water,
1 cup of sugar,
2 lemons,
3 oranges,
1 package of gelatine.

DIRECTIONS:—Dissolve the gelatine in one cup of cold water; extract the juice from the lemons and oranges; strain through a jelly bag; heat until hot, then add the other cup of water and turn into molds; serve with fruits; put in before it sets; use bananas and oranges, or some candied cherries; slice oranges and bannaas thin.

PINEAPPLE MOUSSE.

1 good sized pineapple,
1 cup of sugar,
3 tablespoons of brandy,
1 quart of good cream.

DIRECTIONS:—Pare and cut three-fourths of the pineapple; put in a chopping bowl, pound very fine; pass through a sieve; whip your cream; next add the sugar and brandy to the apple; add the cream last; put in a freezer and freeze; garnish with the remainder of the apple. This will be found delicious on hot days.

APPLE SNOW.

5 large apples,
1½ cups of sugar,
2 eggs,
1 teaspoon of lemon.

DIRECTIONS:—Pare and quarter the apples; stew done and mash fine; pass through a colander; add the sugar and beat the whites of the two eggs; add flavoring and whip until very light and serve heaped in a glass dish with cream.

Hot and Cold Drinks.

COFFEE, NO. 1.

2 quarts of boiling water,
¼ pound of ground coffee,
1 egg.

DIRECTIONS:—Beat the egg up well; add to the coffee; stir well; let stand awhile, then add a little cold water, then the boiling water; let boil five minutes; strain into a china coffee-pot (or silver); keep in a warm place till ready to serve. A very nice way is to grind your coffee and weigh and measure it; afterwards it is no trouble in making your coffee.

TO MAKE GOOD COFFEE NO. 2.

One cup of ground coffee; one half of an egg; mix the egg thoroughly with the coffee; put a small amount of water on and let it set on the back of the stove for a half an hour; then pour to this six cups of boiling hot water; let it boil for five minutes, stirring it several times while boiling, as it makes better coffee to stir it often while boiling; when boiled this length of time, set it back on the stove and it is ready to serve and will be as clear as amber.

DELICIOUS CHOCOLATE, NO 1.

2 tablespoons of chocolate,
5 cups of water,
3 tablespoons of sugar,
1 egg.

DIRECTIONS.—Dissolve the chocolate in a little warm water; put into a kettle, with five cups of water; beat the whole egg up; add the sugar and the egg; stir enough to mix; let simmer, but do not let it boil. Is nice to serve with toast; some like chocolate flavored with rose extract or lemon, but is very nice without.

TO MAKE GOOD CHOCOLATE, NO. 2.

The first thing requisite to making good chocolate is to purchase only the best quality; allow only one-fourth of an ounce of chocolate to each person; to every fourth of an ounce allow one large cup of hot water and one cup of new milk; heat them and scrape the chocolate in and mix well, let it come to the boiling point and serve immediately with loaf sugar. Made exactly by this it will be found excellent.

TO MAKE GOOD TEA.

To make tea for six persons, allow one teaspoon of tea to each pint of hot water; put in an earthen tea-pot; let stand for twenty minutes and serve; keep the the tea-pot very hot.

RASPBERRY WATER.

Take one quart of raspberries; mash them and strain; add the juice from one lemon, two cups of white sugar and five cups of water; stir till the sugar dissolves; then bottle for use. It can be diluted with water, but is not too strong. It should be set on ice at least one hour before serving.

PEACH WATER.

Use one pint of peach jam, one-half cup of sweet almonds, after pounding them to a morter, one cup of sugar, juice of four lemons, one quart of water; strain and it is ready to use.

CURRANT WATER.

One quart of very ripe currants, taken off the stem, one quart of water, one pint of sugar and juice of three lemons; strain and bottle and it is ready to use.

STRAWBERRY WATER.

One pint of berries, one lemon, two cups of sugar, one pint of water; mash the berries; add the lemon juice, sugar and water; strain through a jelly bag and bottle. Is very nice served ice cold.

A NICE CHERRY DRINK

Take very ripe cherries, the Morrillas are the best; put them in a bowl, and after being pitted, mash with the hands; then strain; to two pints of juice add one cup of lemon juice, three cups of sugar and one quart of water; mix well together, and it is ready to serve.

RASPBERRY SHRUB.

Take a half gallon of ripe berries; cover with cider vinegar; let stand for about two days; then strain through a jelly bag, and to every cup of juice, add one cup of white sugar; then put on the stove in a granite iron kettle and cook for one-half an hour; when cool, bottle and cork; must be kept in a dark, cool place; allow one cup of this to one-half gallon of ice water. Is a very nice drink.

TO MAKE LEMONADE.

Allow four lemons to two quarts of ice water, and one pint of white sugar; roll until they are soft; use a lemon squeezer, if one can be had, as with one, the juice can be more easily extracted from the lemons, and more thoroughly, as well; mix and let stand on ice awhile, and it is ready to serve.

PEACH ICE CREAM.

1½ quarts of cream,
1½ pints of peaches,
2 cups of sugar,
2 whole eggs,
1 pint of water.

DIRECTIONS:—Boil the water and sugar together for at least five minutes; pass the peaches through a colander, then add them to the syrup; then the beaten eggs; cook for five minutes, stir constantly; then take from the fire and place in cold water; whip the cream and add when cold and freeze; pack to ripen. Serve with peach short cake.

PLAIN ICE CREAM.

½ gallon of new milk,
1 quart of cream,
4 eggs,
2 teacups of sugar,
1 tablespoon of vanilla.

DIRECTIONS:—Beat the eggs separately; add the sugar to the yolks of the eggs; beat till light, then add the milk; put in a double boiler, cook three minutes, then remove and let cool; whip the cream and add to the milk; then the beaten whites of the eggs and flavoring and it is ready to freeze.

ICE COFFEE.

Make some coffee very strong; strain into an earthen pitcher; let cool, then set on ice till wanted to serve; put some cracked ice in each glass.

TO MAKE ICE TEA.

Make as for other tea, only a little stronger; cool as directed for coffee; set on ice and serve with cracked ice, same as for coffee. So many wait till almost ready to serve coffee or tea and then attempt to get it cold enough by putting ice in, and it makes it too weak and is not fit to drink.

Creams and Ices.

RUSSIAN CREAM.

½ package of gelatine,
1 quart of milk,
3 eggs,
2 small cups of sugar,
1 tablespoon of vanilla.

DIRECTIONS:—Soak gelatine in enough water to cover it, for four hours; scald the milk; remove from the stove; let cool a little; add the beaten yolks, sugar and gelatine; stir while mixing; return to the fire; boil five minutes, stirring constantly; remove again and stir in the beaten whites; add the flavoring; strain and put in a mold wet with cold water. Eat cold, with sauce if preferred.

NEW YORK ICE CREAM.

2 quarts of cream,
1 large cup of sugar,
2 teaspoons of strawberry flavoring.

DIRECTIONS.—Whip the cream about one-half the time you would for desserts; add the sugar before you begin to whip the cream; then add the flavoring just before putting in the freezer. This will be found excellent if made exactly by recipe.

GINGER DRINK.

To a glass of ice water; stir in one tablespoon of vinegar and two tablespoons of sugar, and about one-fourth teaspoon of ginger. This is a very invigorating drink in warm weather.

OATMEAL DRINK.

1 pound of oatmeal,
½ cup of white sugar,
1 lemon,
1 gallon of hot water.

DIRECTIONS:—Put in a porcelain kettle the oatmeal, sugar and juice of the lemon with a little water; mix well and add the gallon of hot water; set on ice till cold and serve.

NECTAR.

5 oranges,
3 lemons,
1 can of pineapples.
2 quarts of water,
2 cups of sugar.

DIRECTIONS:—Extract the juice from the lemon and oranges; add the sugar and juice of the can of pineapples; last the water; stir all together and put in pieces of broken ice; when very cold, serve.

STRAWBERRY AND LEMON ICE.

1 pound of white sugar,
1½ large cups of cold water,
1 quart of strawberry juice,
1 lemon.

DIRECTIONS.—Boil sugar and water together until thick; remove from stove and add juice of lemon and strawberries; put in a freezer and freeze.

LEMON ICE.

6 lemons,
3 cups of sugar,
4 quarts of water,
¼ ounce of gelatine.

DIRECTIONS.—Squeeze the juice from the lemons; add the sugar; then dissolve the gelatine in boiling water; add this: strain and freeze. This is very nice.

GRAPE ICE.

2 cups of ripe grapes,
2 pounds of sugar,
2 quarts of water,
Whites of 5 eggs,
2 lemons.

DIRECTIONS.—Wash the grapes; squeeze the juice from the lemons and add to grapes; strain through a jelly bag and add the sugar; put in a freezer and freeze; add eggs, whisked light, when about half frozen.

NEAPOLITAN ICE.

1 pint of raspberry ice,
1 pint of lemon ice,
1 pint of strawberry ice,
1 pint of orange ice,
1 pint of pineapple ice.

DIRECTIONS.—Make the ices by any recipe for ices; after all is frozen, but not too stiff, remove each one as it is frozen; put in a mold or flat pan; when one of the light ices is put in, put the raspberry then one of the light ones, then the strawberry; last a light one; pack close together, by pressing down, set the mold on ice and set away for several hours to ripen; when ready to serve slice like cake. This makes a beautiful ice.

FRUIT ICE CREAM.

Make as any ordinary cream; squeeze the juice from the fruit and add the sugar; mix well; add to the milk; whip the cream as in other creams; add this and freeze. The juice from several kinds of fruit makes an excellent cream.

CHOCOLATE ICE CREAM.

Make as you would the plain cream, but reserve one cup of sugar, melt the sugar with one-fourth cup of water, and one cup of grated chocolate, by setting the pan in hot water and stirring till it looks smooth; when cold add the flavoring; mix with the cream and freeze.

ORANGE ICE.

5 oranges,
1 lemon,
3 cups of sugar,
3 quarts of water.

DIRECTIONS:—Extract the juice from the oranges and lemon; add the sugar and water; put in a freezer and freeze until very stiff; remove dash and beat with a paddle till smooth; pack in ice at least half a day.

STRAWBERRY BAVARIAN CREAM.

2 tablespoons of gelatine,
1 quart of ripe berries,
2 cups of sugar,
1 cup of water,
2 cups of cream.

DIRECTIONS:—Soak the gelatine in the cup of cold water; soak half an hour; mash the berries; add the sugar and strawberries and set the gelatine over boiling water after it is dissolved; then strain through a cloth and add to the other; add the cream last. Set on ice until very cold.

LEMON ICE CREAM.

2 lemons,
2 large cups of sugar,
½ gallon of new milk,
1 pint of cream.

DIRECTIONS:—Squeeze the juice from the lemons; add to the sugar and put on a stove to heat till well blended together; then cool and add to the milk and whip the cream and add this to the other and freeze.

FRENCH CREAM.

1 quart of new milk,
½ of a box of gelatine,
4 eggs,
5 tablespoons of sugar,
1 teaspoon of vanilla.

DIRECTIONS.—Dissolve the gelatine in one-half of the milk; put almost all of the remainder of the milk in a boiler or kettle and heat until it comes to a boil; then stir the gelatine and milk into this; beat the eggs separately; add the milk that was left and stir the yolks in; flavor with the vanilla; mix well; whip and put in a mold; pour the mixture in on the whites and they will rise to the top; set on ice or a cool place and when cold the clear gelatine will be next to the last and whites on top. Serve with any good sauce or cream.

BAKED ICE CREAM.

This quite a novelty. Make a rich puff paste; roll out the usual thickness; freeze the cream till it is frozen as much as it can be frozen; then make into balls and put one ball into each piece of pastry rolled out; roll as for dumplings, have it all ready, also the pan to bake them in, before making the cream into balls; put the cream in and wet the edges of the crust and enclose lightly; put in a quick oven and immediately they are done; serve at once. It is quite a novelty, indeed; for if done as quick as possible the surprise will be that the cream is melted but very little.

ICE CREAM,—EXCELLENT.

3 quarts of rich cream,
2 whole eggs,
1 cup of white sugar,
¼ teaspoon of soda,—very scant,
3 teaspoons of vanilla.

DIRECTIONS:—First whip the cream with the soda added till light, but not stiff; then beat the eggs with the sugar and flavoring; then mix well together and put in the freezer and freeze till well frozen; remove dash and whip lightly with a spoon and pack and set away to ripen at least four hours. This, if made properly, can not be excelled.

TUTTI FRUTTI.

Take one quart of cream, two ounces of sweet almonds; after being chopped fine, add one-half a pound of sugar; mix well together and put in a freezer and freeze about half as much as usually for cream; now mix in one pint of candied strawberries; pack and set away for several hours before serving. This is fine.

LEMON SHERBET.

One cup of lemon juice, two cups of white sugar, three cups of cold water; mix well together and freeze till stiff, but care has to be taken not to freeze too much, as this spoils any kind of ices.

ORANGE SHERBET.

½ gallon of water,
5 oranges,
3 cups of sugar,
2 lemons,
Whites of 3 eggs.

DIRECTIONS.—Extract the juice from the oranges and lemons; add the sugar; beat the whites of the eggs stiff, and add last, after adding the juice and sugar to the water, put in a freezer and freeze. Serve when frozen about half as much as cream.

ROMAN PUNCH.

1 pint of fruit syrup,
1 glass of brandy,
Whites of 3 eggs.

DIRECTIONS.—Take any kind of fruit desired; after extracting the juice, add sugar to make a syrup; then put the brandy in, and have the freezer ready; put in and freeze until about half frozen; then add the whites of the eggs, whipped stiff, and proceed to finishing freezing. Should be frozen as any other ices.

CRIMSON SHERBET

Two cups of strawberry juice, one cup of lemon juice, one pint of granulated sugar, two pints of cold water; add water and sugar and boil for five minutes; then remove, and when cool add the juice of the fruit and strain through a jelly bag; put in a freezer and freeze; remove the dasher and pack till wanted to serve. The white of an egg to this amount, beaten stiff, and added to a cup of sugar, is an addition, putting in after it has been frozen, before it is packed.

CANDY MAKING AT HOME.

CANDY MAKING.

It seems as though it would be a difficult task, but if properly managed, will not fail to give satisfaction, and the following recipes will be found sufficent to give a variety of candies, and they all are excellent, if made exactly by the recipes given. Glucose enters largely into nearly all candies. It is simply syrup made from corn, and if needed, can be procured from any confectioner. The pans used to boil candy in should either be granite, or porcelain lined, and there will be no coloring from the pan.

TO MAKE MARSH MALLOWS.

¼ pound of loaf sugar,
¼ pound of gum arabic,
1 cup of water,
Whites of 2 egg.

DIRECTIONS.—Add the gum arabic to the water; dissolve thoroughly, and strain: add the sugar to this; put on the stove; stir until the sugar is dissolved; now add the whites of the eggs, well beaten: stir in gradually: stir till the mixture seems thin; and it will not adhere to the fingers; pour in pans; sprinkle with corn starch; cut in squares, and dip in powdered sugar.

A GOOD HOARHOUND CANDY.

2 pints of water,
2 ounces of dried hoarhound,
3 pounds of brown sugar.

DIRECTIONS:—Put the hoarhound in the water, boil until the strength is extracted from the hoarhound; then strain, and add the sugar; boil until it is very brittle, but do not stir; pour into buttered tins, and when almost cold cut in sticks or squares. This is fine.

TO MAKE NUT CARAMELS.

These are made as other caramels, except just before removing from the stove the meats from hickory nuts are added; in fact any kind of nut meats are nice for this candy; do not stir only enough to mix the meats properly with the candy; pour on buttered plates and cut in small pieces or in sticks. Peanut candy is nice made in this way.

CREAM TAFFY.

1½ cups of white sugar,
¼ cup of vinegar,
¼ cup of water,
1 small piece of butter,
1 teaspoon of strawberry flavoring.

DIRECTIONS:—Put the sugar, water and vinegar together; add the butter, a piece the size of a walnut will be sufficient; boil till if put in cold water it will be brittle; pour in plates, and pull till it is very white; cut in sticks.

A GOOD TAFFY.

1 pint of molasses,
¼ pound of butter,
¼ cup of good vinegar.

DIRECTIONS.—Boil the molasses and butter together till it begins to thicken; then add the vinegar; cook till it is brittle, by putting in cold water; pour on plates and when partly cool proceed to pull it; butter or flour the hands. This makes a rich taffy.

CHOCOLATE CARAMELS.

2 cups of brown sugar,
⅔ cup of grated chocolate,
1 small cup of cold water,
1 tablespoon of vinegar.
1 teaspoon of lemon extract,
1 tablespoon of butter.

DIRECTIONS.—Put sugar, water, chocolate and vinegar on to boil; after it begins to boil add the butter and flavoring. Be careful and not stir any, but when it has boiled for at least twenty minutes try in cold water, and if brittle, pour in plates and cut in small squares.

COCOANUT CREAM CANDY.

2 pounds of white sugar,
1 cup of milk from cocoanut,
1 large cup of grated cocoanut,

DIRECTIONS.—Put the sugar on to boil with the milk from the cocoanut; boil for at least ten minutes; then grate the cup of cocoanut and add; boil for ten minutes; then remove and pour on plates and make into balls or cut in squares. They will be several days drying, but when dry are very good.

BUTTERSCOTCH NO. 2.

2 cups of sugar,
2 cups of molasses,
1 cup of butter,
2 tablespoons of vinegar,
¼ teaspoon of soda.

DIRECTIONS:—Put the ingredients all together and boil till it is well done; pour in plates, cut in squares, and if wanted to be kept any length of time wrap in paraffine paper.

TO MAKE CREAM WALNUTS.

1 lb. of white sugar,
1 cup of water,
1 teaspoon of vanilla.

DIRECTIONS:—Put sugar, vanilla and water together; boil till when put on plates will be creamy; make into small cakes, and have some English walnut kernels ready and press in the top of each two or three kernels; dip in powdered sugar and set aside. When properly made they are fine.

MAPLE CREAMS.

1 lb. of maple sugar,
1 cup of water,
1 piece of butter, size of a walnut,

DIRECTIONS:—Put the sugar and water on to boil; when it boils five minutes add the butter; boil until it begins to harden, then remove from the stove and make into small balls, and put the meats from any kind of nuts desired in between two balls; lay on buttered tins to harden.

CHOCOLATE CREAMS.

3 cups of pulverized sugar,
1 cup of good cream,
1 tablespoon of vanilla,
1 cup of grated chocolate.

DIRECTIONS.—Put the cream and sugar on to boil; let it boil for five minutes; then flavor and remove from the stove; as soon as it is cool enough, make into balls; put the chocolate in a pan and set over boiling water until it is melted thoroughly; then dip each ball into the chocolate and lay on a buttered plate to harden; these, if properly made, are excellent.

CHOCOLATE CREAMS, NO. 2.

½ pound of loaf sugar;
1 cup of cream
¼ pound of vanilla chocolate,
1 teaspoon of strawberry flavoring.

DIRECTIONS.—Put all the ingredients into a granite iron pan; put the chocolate on in a pan over hot water to melt; cook the cream till it hardens readily in cold water; pour into a deep plate or dish; beat till it is cold, but it must not be stirred any while boiling; make into balls or squares; dip in the melted chocolate and lay on buttered plates to cool. Do not boil the cream too long, as this causes it to grain.

BUTTERSCOTCH.

2 pounds of brown sugar,
¼ cup of butter,
1 small teaspoon of cream of tartar,
1 small cup of cold water,
1 teaspoon of vanilla.

DIRECTIONS.—Put the cream of tartar with the sugar and add the water, vinegar and butter; put on to cook; boil till brittle; try by putting a small amount in cold water; add the vanilla last, just before taking from the stove; pour on plates and cut in squares.

GOOD BUTTER TAFFY.

1 cup of sugar,
1 cup of water,
1 lump of butter the size of a walnut,
2 large tablespoons of vinegar,
½ teaspoon of lemon extract,
¼ teaspoon of soda.

DIRECTIONS:—Put sugar and water on to boil, also the vinegar; cook about fifteen minutes, then put the butter in and cook till it will harden easily in cold water; stir the lemon in quickly and put on buttered plates to cool. Is very nice rolled or cut in squares.

LEMON CANDY.

2 cups of white sugar,
1 large cup of water,
2 teaspoons of vinegar,
1 lemon.

DIRECTIONS:—Add the sugar, water and vinegar together; cook without stirring for half an hour; then add the lemon juice and cook till it will harden in cold water; pour on buttered plates and before it has time to harden, press some walnuts or any kind of nuts preferred into it as far apart as the squares are to be cut. This is very nice.

Canned and Dried Fruits.

A FEW REMARKS ON CANNING.

The only art in canning is to be careful in selecting your fruit for this purpose. Only fresh, sound fruit should ever be used for canning purposes. In canning small fruits, such as currants, they should be carefully removed from the stem, and washed before removing from stem. In preparing cherries for canning, remove the pits, but the flavor is much improved by cracking some of them and adding a few to each can. Berries of any kind should be sound and if washed should be put in a sieve or colander and water poured over them, as they need not be handled in this way. In preparing pineapple, remove the eyes carefully, as this spoils the appearance if any are left in. Peaches should have warm water poured over them, pared and halved, and they should not be over ripe, as this spoils any kind of canned fruit, as well as not to have it ripe enough. To can plums, pour hot water over them and remove the skins, if they are a variety that have tough skins, if not do not remove them, but they should be put in hot water a while to remove that bitter taste that most plums have. Pears should be pared and cut in halves; the air must be entirely excluded from the fruit to insure it keeping well.

TO CAN CHERRIES.

After removing the pits from the cherries put them in a porcelain kettle and to every quart of cherries, put one-half a pound of sugar; cook for five minutes; have the cans dry and hot; heat them by putting in hot water; fill the cans and put a piece of writing paper over the top, after wetting it in brandy, over this put some white sugar and your fruit will never mould.

CANNED PEACHES.

Have only firm, ripe peaches; pare and drop in cold water, in the mean time have the fruit kettle with one cup of water and fill in with peaches and for each quart of fruit allow one half cup of white sugar sprinkled over the fruit; when the kettle is filled, heat it slowly to the boiling point, then boil three minutes and proceed to fill the cans with the peaches; have plenty of syrup on the top as they will keep better; have the cans perfectly dry, as that prevents mould.

TO PUT UP CORN WITH ACID.

Use two ounces of tartaric acid to every pint of water. Cut the corn from the cob, add just enough water to cook it sufficiently. When done add two tablespoons of acid solution to every quart of corn. Put in the cans and seal immediately, and put in a dry, cool place. When using add one-fourth teaspoon of soda to each quart of corn. Let it stand for several minutes before putting on to cook. Never cook corn in tin. Season with butter, salt and cream. Beans and peas can be put up the same way.

TO CAN EGG PLANT.

Peel and slice them; lay in cold water slightly salted; fill the cans and add about one pint of cold water; proceed to seal and cook as above. The plant is very nice to cook in winter, and helps to furnish a variety.

TO CAN SQUASH.

Choose a good mealy squash for canning; cut in rather small pieces and boil till well done and mash and fill the cans; have the cans very hot and seal immediately and put away in a cool place.

TO CAN CORN.

After husking the corn, remove the silks carefully, then cut the corn from the cob; pack closely in the cans; screw the tops on and do not add any water; proceed as in canning tomatoes or beans; when cold see that the tops are on as tight as they can be made and wrap them in paper and keep in a dark, dry place.

TO CAN BEANS.

Choose tender beans and cut in small pieces as for cooking; fill the cans and add water till the cans will be full, then put the top on and screw tight; put in the water and boil for three hours, let remain in the water till cold and again examine the cans and see that they are perfectly tight. Close attention is all that is needed to insure success in canning at home.

TO CAN STRAWBERRIES.

If they are free from sand and dirt do not wash them, as they are nicer and do not cook up so much; weigh the berries, and allow one pound of sugar to four pounds of berries; put sugar in a porcelain kettle; add one cup of water, and when it boils add the berries; let cook a few minutes; then dip out into cans, and strain the syrup in; have enough syrup to cover them well; wrap each can in paper: keep in a dark, cool place.

A NICE WAY TO PUT UP BERRIES READY FOR THE TABLE.

Take any kind of berries; pick them over; wash and drain them; make a rather weak syrup: keep it hot; put the berries in the cans; set them in cold water; after they have been in the water for fifteen minutes after it begins to boil, pour the syrup over them; let remain for fifteen minutes longer; then remove and seal them. They are very nice and have a good flavor.

PEACHES PUT UP IN BRANDY.

Choose perfectly sound peaches; drop in hot water to remove the roughness of the peach, and let remain a few minutes; then dry them on a cloth; put on in a kettle; for every pound of peaches put one pound of loaf sugar, one pint of water, one-half pint of good brandy; boil and skim the syrup; then pour over the peaches in a stone jar; heat for nine mornings; then heat the syrup and add the peaches; cook twenty minutes, briskly; put in jars and seal. They are ready for use in about a month.

ANOTHER METHOD OF CANNING PEACHES.

Choose nice ripe peaches; pare and halve them; put in glass jars, and have syrup made and poured over them; set them in cold water and let cook sufficiently done; remove and seal; wrap brown paper around the cans. Canned in this way, they are very nice.

PEARS.

Peel and halve them; put in a steamer and cook over boiling water till tender, then put in jars; have a thin syrup made and strained; pour this over while boiling hot; seal and keep in a dark place. These are fine.

TO CAN PEACHES BY THE COLD PROCESS.

Pare the peaches and halve them and put in the cans; have ready some syrup made of white sugar and water, boiled till well dissolved; pour enough of this over to cover the peaches; set away to allow the syrup to settle down in the cans, and fill again. This time seal and put in a dark, dry place. If not kept from the light they will not keep as well. In canning this way only perfectly sound fruit should be used.

TO CAN TOMATOES.

Put the tomatoes in a steamer until the skins can be easily removed; slice in rather thick slices; put in glass jars; put the top on and screw tightly; put something in a wash boiler to keep the cans from being immediately on the bottom; then set the cans in and fill with cold water, almost to the top—about up to the lid; boil for at least two hours; do not let the water cease boiling; remove boiler from the fire, and do not take the cans from the boiler until the water is cold.

AMOUNT OF SUGAR FOR CANNED FRUITS.

To can any kind of small fruits ready for the table the amount of sugar for each quart of fruit is as follows:

Pineapple, ¼ pound,
Siberian Crab, ½ pound,
Apples, ½ pound,
Plums, 1 pound,
Apricots, 1 pound,
Currants, ¾ pound,
Cherries, ½ pound,
Raspberries, ½ pound,
Quinces, ½ pound,
Strawberries, ½ pound,
Pears, ¼ pound,
Peaches, ½ pound,
Blackberries, ½ pound.

TO DRY CHERRIES AND PLUMS.

Remove the pits from them and sprinkle sugar over them; set in the oven for at least half a day and then they can be put in the sun to finish drying. They are very nice when dried for mince pies and for puddings; are nice to garnish with if let dry about half then put in stone jars, a layer of fruit then a layer of sugar, and will be convenient to use at any time.

DRIED PEACHES.

Take very ripe peaches, cut them in halves, and expose to the hot sun until thoroughly dried; they should be protected from the flies by stretching a mosquito bar over them, and all fruit should be treated in the same way while drying; it requires several days for peaches to dry.

TO DRY BLACKBERRIES AND RASPBERRIES.

Pick the berries carefully, and put in a cool oven long enough to dry all the juice from around them; then put on a cloth in the hot sun for several days; on putting out in the morning stir them up well, as by this means they will be dried all through alike. All small fruits can be dried in this way.

TO DRY APPLES.

Pare and quarter them; put on a cloth or board in the hot sun; cover them as any other fruit, with mosquito bar, as this insures them from flies and dust; it will require several days to dry apples; when dried they can be put away in sacks or boxes for future use.

DRIED GRAPES.

Pick nice ripe grapes; put on a cloth in the hot sun, or can be dried in the stove, but are nicer sun dried. Dry until perfectly dry or they will mould.

GRAPES IN SUGAR.

Pick only sound grapes; dry partly in the sun; then pack in a jar; a layer of grapes and one of brown sugar. Do not pick the grapes from the stem; cover with two inches of sugar on top. When properly dried they are as nice as raisins.

Miscellaneous Recipes.

TO SERVE DIFFERENT KINDS OF FRUIT.

GRAPES:—Grapes should be pulled when nicely ripe; select large bunches and arrange in a tall glass dish with a few grape leaves around the edge as a garnish.

PEACHES:—Choose nice ripe peaches, but not too ripe, as they do not look so nice; they are much nicer on plates; pull some with a leaf or two attached.

CHERRIES:—Cherries should be pulled if possible with the stem, and as many cherries attached to one stem as can be, as they look very pretty in a glass dish, also with some of the leaves.

WATERMELON:—Put the melon in a refrigerator until thoroughly chilled; when ready to serve remove and cut roundways, put on plates and send to the table; or some prefer to serve them with the rind cut away and eaten with an orange spoon.

CANTALOUPES:—Cantaloupes are well chilled before serving, same as the melons, but not sliced as melons, they are sliced length-wise; pepper and salt each slice; arrange on plates and serve,

ORANGES:—Oranges are nice cut in halves, and served on small plates and eaten with an orange spoon; or sliced thin, sprinkled with sugar, and let stand several hours on ice. Are very nice both ways.

BERRIES OF ANY KIND:—Pick carefully, removing all stems; lay in a colander and pour water over them, in order not to bruise the fruit by handling too much; let them drain, then put in a fruit or berry dish; sprinkle liberally with sugar, and set on ice until ready to serve; can be served with cake and cream or alone.

CORN MOCK OYSTERS.

2 cups of grated corn,
½ cup of milk,
½ cup of flour,
1 tablespoon of butter,
2 eggs,
1 teaspoon of salt,
¼ teaspoon of pepper.

DIRECTIONS.—Grate the corn from the cob; whisk the eggs and add; then add the milk, salt and pepper; sift in the flour; have ready the frying pan with some butter, (same as for frying oysters;) drop in a large spoonful of the dough; fry until brown, turn on the other side; serve on hot plates. These will be found nearly as good as oysters.

HINTS ON THE HOME DAIRY.

In setting the milk, as soon as it is strained it is a good plan to set it in cold water, if ice cannot be procured; forty degrees temperature is about right to raise cream perfectly; there should never be more than one inch of milk in one pan, as the cream raises more quickly; the cream should not be skimmed when wanted, for churning purposes under twenty-four hours, and when skimmed into a jar should be well stirred two or three times a day, and when evenly soured through and slightly acid it is ready to churn and in making good butter there should never be any water put in while churning, but if too cool set in warm water and let stand awhile till it is the right heat. The too common practice of scalding the cream renders the butter unfit for use; also the salting of the butter is often spoiled by using coarse salt and not being careful to roll it to mash all the lumps. The butter ought to be worked thoroughly twice, and this will insure no milk or streaks that is so often found in butter, which makes it unsaleable.

TAPIOCA CREAM.

2 tablespoons of tapioca,
3 eggs
1 quart of milk,
1 small cup of sugar,
1 teaspoon of vanilla.

DIRECTIONS:—Cover the tapioca with cold water; let stand over night, then pour the water off and add the milk; put on the stove and stir in the yolks of the eggs; let it boil two minutes; add the sugar and flavoring; remove, and when nearly cold, add the beaten whites of the eggs; mix lightly and serve in custard glasses.

STEAMED RICE.

1 cup of rice,
3 cups of hot water,
1 pinch of salt.

DIRECTIONS:—Wash the rice; put in a small pan and set in a steamer over a kettle of boiling water; after it is cooked almost done, add salt; in this way the grains are preserved whole and looks very nice and white. Serve with sauce.

MACARONI WITH BUTTER.

Boil the macaroni till tender in weak salt water; put on a plate; take one large tablespoon of butter; put in the stove to melt; first grate some cheese over the macaroni, then pour over the melted butter and serve at once. This is very nice.

CORN CUSTARD.

4 large ears of corn,
1 cup of sweet milk,
3 eggs,
2 tablespoons of butter,
¼ teaspoon of black pepper,
1 teaspoon of salt.

DIRECTIONS:—Cut the corn from the cob; whisk the eggs until light, add them to the corn; then the milk, salt, pepper and butter; butter a baking dish and after mixing well, put in and bake half an hour in a moderate oven. You will find this a very nice way to cook corn. When green corn is not in season, canned corn will do nicely.

BUTTER CUPS.

8 eggs,
1 teaspoon of butter.
1 teaspoon of mustard,
½ teaspoon of pepper,
1 teaspoon of salt,
1 cup of chicken,
1 cup of ham,
½ of an onion,
2 tablespoons of bread crumbs,
1 cup of gravy.

DIRECTIONS:—Boil eggs hard; cut a small piece off the end of egg and remove the yolk; set the whites in a baking dish powder the yolks with mustard, salt and onion chopped fine and melted butter, bread crumbs, minced chicken, ham; add the pepper and enough gravy to moisten it; roll into balls size of yolks put one ball into each of the whites of the eggs; pour over with gravy a bit of butter on each one and sprinkle a little cracker meal over and send to oven and bake until nicely browned. Will require ten or fifteen minutes to bake.

STEWED APPLES.

½ dozen apples,
1 large cup of sugar,
1 lemon,
1 pint of water.

DIRECTIONS.—Pare and quarter the apples; pour the hot water over them; add the sugar; cook slow until clear; then remove, and when cold put in a glass dish; add the lemon juice just before serving; garnish with thin slices of lemon.

A WELCH DISH.

¼ pound of good cheese,
½ cup of milk,
½ teaspoon of mustard,
½ teaspoon of salt,
1 pinch of cayenne,
1 tablespoon of butter,
5 slices of toast.

DIRECTIONS.—Grate the cheese; add to the milk, and put in a kettle; mix mustard, cayenne and eggs together; beat well; when the cheese melts put into the mixture and add the butter; cook not more than three minutes; toast the bread and pour over; serve while hot.

MACAROONS

2 small cups of flour,
½ cup of butter,
1 cup of sugar,
1 egg.

DIRECTIONS.—Mix well together; make into small cakes and dip in sugar; put in a pan and bake in a moderate oven until a delicate brown.

TO COOK BARLEY.

Wash the barley well; put to cook in warm water, but do not have it hot; let it boil a few minutes; then pour off and put fresh water over again; cook slowly for at least three hours, and sometimes it requires a little longer. Barley is served as rice.

BOILED RICE.

Wash the rice well; put to cook in plenty of water, boiling hot. It requires a long time to cook rice properly, and as it swells so much in cooking. It is not necessary to cook more than a cupful for a good sized family, it cooks better, and is nicer to cook in a double boiler, as it is very white and the grains are whole when done. It may be served plain or seasoned with salt and butter, and some like cream added.

CHEESE STRAWS.

Four tablespoons of flour, four tablespoons of cheese, two tablespoons of butter, one teaspoon of salt, two tablespoons of milk, one-half teaspoon of pepper—use cayenne pepper, one-fourth teaspoon of nutmeg, two yolks of eggs; melt the butter; beat the yolks; add to the butter; sift the flour; add the nutmeg, pepper, salt and grated cheese; to this add the eggs, butter and milk; mix and roll out; cut in strips; bake in a slow oven; serve with any kind of salads.

TO MAKE PREPARED MUSTARD.

Two tablespoons of ground mustard, one of flour, one teaspoon of sugar; mix the flour, mustard and sugar together; then pour enough boiling water over to make a stiff paste; let cool; then add cold vinegar till it is the consistency desired.

CHEESE SOUFFLE.

1 cup of bread crumbs,
½ cup of sweet milk,
5 tablespoons of cheese,
3 eggs,
1 pinch of salt and pepper,

DIRECTIONS.—Put the milk on the stove; let raise a boil; put bread crumbs in; beat smooth; add cheese, after grating, and add salt, pepper, and yolks beaten light; whip the whites and add last; butter a dish and bake in a hot oven for about fifteen minutes; serve warm.

BAKED CHEESE AND RICE.

Take one pint of rice, which has been cooked tender, one cup of grated cheese; grease a pan; put some rice in, then cheese, salt, butter, and a pinch of pepper, rice and cheese till all is used; put about one cup of new milk over and set in the oven and bake twenty minutes; serve while hot.

PLAIN CORN MUSH.

Sift meal, and have a kettle of hot water, and salt it to taste; then sift the meal in, a little at a time, until it is moderately thick, but not too thick, as that spoils it, for it should cook at least one-half an hour; stir often, as that makes the mush smooth, which adds to the appearance, as well as the taste; serve with butter or cream.

FRIED MUSH.

Have the mush cold; slice in slices about one inch thick; dip in meal and fry in lard until crisp and brown; lay on a platter and garnish with mutton chops.

FRENCH FRIED MUSH.

Take any light corn bread; remove the crust; add some warm water; soak a few minutes; then add a pinch of salt and pepper; have some nice fresh fat in a frying pan; add a little water; stir the bread in; let remain about five minutes; dish up and serve while hot.

GRAHAM MUSH.

Put some water in a kettle, and salt it a little; stir in enough graham flour till it thickens enough; cook till it is well done, as any kind of mush needs to be cooked well, as it is easy to have a raw taste; serve with cream and butter.

PEACH FRITTERS.

1 quart of flour,
1 pint of milk,
2 tablespoons of butter,
1 large teaspoon of salt,
3 eggs,
½ cup of sugar,
2 cups of sliced peaches,
½ teaspoon of soda,
1 teaspoon of cream of tartar.

DIRECTIONS:—Sift flour and cream of tartar together; melt the butter slightly; whip the eggs light and add; dissolve soda in hot water and last add the peaches dredged well with the sugar; drop by spoonfuls in boiling lard; cook till brown; remove and sprinkle with sugar. Serve while warm.

SALTED ALMONDS.

Blanch them by laying in hot water a few minutes, when the inside hull or skin can be easily removed, and to one pint of the almonds, allow one tablespoon of melted butter and one teaspoon of salt; mix well and put in a shallow pan; set in the oven and brown; it will take about fifteen or twenty minutes; must not have the oven too hot; remove to a plate and cool. These will be much nicer than those purchased at the confectioner's, because they are fresh.

TO COOK HOMINY.

Take a quart of hominy; put on in enough water to cover it and cook for several hours as it takes quite awhile to cook as tender as it should be; when done salt and season with meat fryings, or it may be served with butter.

MACARONI.

Boil the macaroni in enough water to cook it tender; then drain and put in a dish and grate some nice cheese over it and then put some pieces of butter over it; salt and pepper it; heat a cup of cream and pour over and serve at once.

TO MAKE PEACH LEATHER.

Take very ripe peaches; split them in the side; remove the seed; spread them out and sprinkle with sugar and put in the sun and dry; when dried sufficiently, roll up and put in jars. Is very nice to use in winter.

TO CANDY FRUITS.

Cook the fruits in very thick syrup; let it stand in the syrup for three days; skim out and lay on plates and sift sugar over and let stand in the sun. Following these directions, any kind of fruit can be candied without difficulty. They are nice served at the table as well as useful in preparing many articles of food, especially nice for mince pies and some kinds of cake, also confectionery.

TOMATO FIGS.

Peel small pear tomatoes; scald them slightly so the peel can be easily removed; put on dishes, sprinkle with sugar, set in a cool oven, just warm enough to bear the hand; when dry on one side, turn and sprinkle with sugar and so on until they are as dry as you want, then pack in sugar.

MADE MUSTARD

1 quart of hot water,
1 quart of vinegar,
¼ pound of best mustard,
1 tablespoon of flour,
¼ teaspoon of salt,
1 teaspoon of sugar.

DIRECTIONS.—Mix all well together, the mustard, sugar and salt, then add the water and vinegar; boil one-half an hour; bottle and seal. This makes fine mustard for meats.

A GOOD BRINE FOR MEATS.

3 gallons of water,
1 quart of rock salt,
1 tablespoon of saltpetre,
1 cup of molasses,
1 cup of brown sugar.

DIRECTIONS:—Mix all together; boil and skim, now pour over the meat and let it remain for four weeks, then remove and smoke them. They are very nice and will be as sweet and fresh in six months as when first taken out of the brine.

Preserves, Jells and Jams.

To make preserves, jells or any kind of jams successfully, the first thing requisite for the success of any thing of this kind is to use only the best sugar, as an inferior quality means a failure in your undertaking. In making preserves, use pound for pound, and in jelly or most fruits that are too acid, three cups of sugar to four of fruit juice is sufficient, and in jellies, a small quantity made at a time is much better than a large one, as the jell will be more clear; always have the glasses warm and dry that you pour your jell into as this prevents moulding. Anything of this kind is better put in glass and kept well sealed. Always skim your syrup well, either preserves or jell, as it will not be strong and more clear than not to attend to this closely. The preparation of the fruit has been given in each recipe and if directions are followed, success will most assuredly be the result.

CITRON PRESERVES.

Pare and cut citron in fancy shapes; put in weak syrup; put on the stove with one lemon sliced to every two pounds of citron, cook until they are tender; then remove and have ready a syrup made by adding as many pounds of sugar as you have fruit; put the fruit in and boil slowly till it is clear; skim out into jars and add some ginger root; boil the syrup ten minutes longer and pour over the preserves and seal.

PEACH PRESERVES

Pare and remove the stones from the peaches; put in cold water immediately, to keep them from turning dark; when all are peeled weigh your fruit, and to every pound of peaches take one pound of sugar; add water enough to make a good syrup; a good proportion will be to cook peaches, as some of them are a little hard to cook, allow one pint of water to each pound of sugar; boil and skim the syrup; now put in the peaches and cook them slowly till they look clear and are tender; remove to jars, boil the syrup five minutes and pour over them and seal.

GRAPE PRESERVES.

Remove the seeds, by squeezing them with the fingers; that will also remove the skins; put the skins in one pan and the pulp in another; measure both the skins and pulp, and allow one cup of white sugar to every cup of fruit; put the sugar on, and put the syrup from the grapes, instead of water; when it has been boiled for about one-half an hour add the fruit and cook for one-half an hour again; skim the preserves out and strain the syrup over and seal.

DAMSON PRESERVES.

Remove the seed, by making an incision in the side of the plum and putting in a steamer and heating awhile, when the seeds can be easily removed; now weigh, and for every pound of fruit allow one of loaf sugar; boil and skim the sugar and add the plums; cook them till they are tender and look clear; remove and put in glass jars and strain the syrup over them. If made properly, damson preserves can not be excelled for richness and fine flavor.

PRUNE PRESERVES.

Put the prunes on, after washing them, and cook till they can be pitted easily; then after pitting them put on in syrup and cook until they are well done; add while cooking, some lemon juice, but if preferred any other flavor can be used; skim out in a jar and pour the syrup over them. The syrup must not be cooked too long or it will have a strong flavor, or incline to jell.

PEAR PRESERVES.

Allow three-fourths of a pound of sugar to one of pears, as they are much sweeter than most kinds of fruit; pare them and cut in halves; after making a syrup, boil about ten minutes; then put your pears in and cook until they look clear. Pear preserves are nicer if steamed before putting in the syrup, same as canning them; when they are cooked enough, put in glass jars and pour the syrup, boiling hot, over them. Pear preserves should not be used for several weeks after they are made.

STRAWBERRY PRESERVES.

Pick the berries a dry day; weigh them, after washing and draining them; weigh the sugar, allowing one pound to every pound of fruit; put on with just enough water to make syrup; boil and skim; add the berries, after putting them in a dish, and setting in the oven and heating until they are hot, so it will not stop the syrup from boiling in putting in the fruit, as they will be nicer not to stop boiling until done; boil gently till the fruit is clear; skim and put in jars; boil the syrup till it begins to thicken; then strain over the fruit. They must be strained so it will take out any seed that might be in the syrup.

ORANGE PRESERVES.

Take ripe oranges, but not too ripe; cut them in pieces about one-fourth of an inch thick; cut round ways and remove the seed; lay in water for several hours; then make a syrup, allowing one pound and a half of sugar to one pound of oranges; put one pint of water to that amount of sugar; boil and skim them; add the oranges and cook for one hour slowly; remove and cook the syrup; adding the juice of one lemon; cook one-half an hour; then strain over the orange. These are fine.

CURRANT PRESERVES.

Pick and wash, not too ripe currants; make a thick syrup; put them in and cook slowly about one-half an hour; then skim them out and cook the syrup ten minutes longer and pour over the currants in jars and seal them up.

CHERRY PRESERVES.

Choose nice large cherries for preserving, and do not have them too ripe, as this, in some varieties, makes strong flavored preserves; stone them carefully; lay in a dish, and make a syrup of good loaf sugar or very nice granulated sugar; wash the cherries in several waters, and drain in a colander; put them in the boiling syrup and boil until they are clear; then remove and put in glass jars; pour the syrup over and seal.

PRESERVED PINEAPPLE.

Pare and quarter the apples; remove the eyes; and to every pound of fruit allow three-quarters of a pound of sugar; boil the syrup for half an hour, then put in the apples; cook till well done and put in glass jars; strain the syrup over while boiling hot and seal.

YELLOW TOMATO PRESERVES.

Scald the tomatoes; after they are cool enough, remove the skins and make a syrup; after boiling for one-half an hour put the tomatoes in, and when they have boiled till they look almost transparent, then put into glass jars; put in the syrup some pieces of ginger root; boil the syrup at least three quarters of an hour; then strain the syrup over the preserves. If care be taken in making this they are fine.

PLUM PRESERVES.

After scalding the plums in water, in which a small piece of soda has been added; remove them, and after cooling stone and weigh, and allow full one pound of sugar for every pound of fruit; put the syrup to cook with enough water to dissolve it well; a good proportion would be, to one pound of sugar, allow one pint of hot water; after the syrup has boiled for fifteen minutes pour over the plums and cover over till the next morning; then strain the syrup into the kettle and boil a while; then put the plums in and cook one-half an hour, rather brisk; skim them out into jars and strain the syrup again over them, after it has boiled ten minutes; after removing the fruit put in glass jars and seal.

QUINCE PRESERVES.

To make nice quince preserves, pare and core them; make a syrup, allowing one pound of sugar to one of fruit; boil and skim the syrup; put the quinces in, after quartering them, if very large, if not halve them; let remain in the syrup, cooking slow until they are cooked through sufficiently; then remove and boil the syrup until it is thick enough, but do not boil too long or it will be dark; strain over the quinces in the jars and seal. They are fine, but must be kept in the dark, although all fruits are better kept in a cool, dark place.

RIPE CUCUMBER PRESERVES.

Gather the cucumbers after they begin to ripen; cut in halves, lay in weak alum water; let remain in this for twenty-four hours, then wash and drain them. Put on in a kettle enough sugar to make a good syrup; cook for about 15 minutes, then put in the cucumbers, after scraping the seeds out; boil them slowly until they are clear; add, while boiling, some slices of lemon peel. When they are done so a fork will pierce them easily remove to jars, and strain the syrup over them and seal. They should not be used for two or three months after making, as age improves them.

WATERMELON PRESERVES.

Cut the melon in square pieces, about one inch square; put in weak alum water; soak over night, then wash them in clear water and make a nice syrup and add one good sized piece of ginger and candied lemon peel; cook till very tender; remove to jars and strain them. Keep three months before using.

BLACKBERRY PRESERVES

Pick the berries when not too ripe; put in a colander and pour water over them; when drained put in a good syrup; put the berries in and cook briskly for one-half an hour; skim out in a jar and boil the syrup ten minutes longer and strain over the berries and seal. Always seal while hot.

GREEN TOMATO PRESERVES.

Use small tomatoes; put them in weak salt water over night; next morning make a good syrup and after it has boiled and been skimmed, add the tomatoes; cook till they can be easily pricked with a fork; then remove and put in jars; put a few slices of lemon in the syrup; boil till it begins to thicken nicely, then pour over the tomatoes and seal.

APPLE PRESERVES, NO. 2.

4 pounds of apples,
2 quarts of water,
1 teaspoonful of ginger,
4 pounds of white sugar,
2 lemons.

DIRECTIONS:—Pare, core and quarter nice preserving apples; weigh them, also the sugar; then add water, sugar and ginger; boil and strain; put in the kettle again and boil five minutes and skim; add the apples; cook until they look clear and are easily pricked with a fork; then remove the apples with a skimmer and strain the syrup again and then boil until it is thick; the lemon is added before straining the last time; cover the apples with a thick cloth when they are taken out so they will not turn dark.

APPLE PRESERVES, NO 1.

Pare and core nice sound apples; quarter them; put in cold water until put to cook; put three-quarters of a pound of sugar to every pound of apples and one lemon to every gallon of preserves; boil the sugar with one quart of water to ¾ pound of sugar; when it boils about ten minutes and is skimmed well, put the apples in and cook till they are tender, then remove and put in glass jars and boil the syrup with the juice of the lemon till it begins to thicken; then strain hot into jars; be sure you have plenty of syrup over the preserves. Sweet apples are the nicest to preserve, although there are other kinds that will make very nice preserves.

NEAPOLITAN JELLY.

Take raspberry, lemon, grape and currant jelly; make in different pans; small pans can be used; after each is done, put in a teacup; when almost cold, put first in a tall jelly glass the grape, then the lemon and currant, last the raspberry, as that is a little lighter in color than the grape. This makes a very pretty glass of jelly as well as nicely flavored.

APPLE JELLY.

Select juicy tart apples; pare and cut in small pieces and put in a kettle and add one pint of water; cook till tender; remove and strain through a thick jelly bag and put back to cook about the same time as other jells and add ¾ of a pound of sugar to each pint of juice; after adding the sugar, cook for two minutes and put in jell glasses; cover with writing paper dipped in the white of an egg.

CARDINAL JELLY.

1 box of gelatine,
2 cups of sugar,
1 cup of cranberry juice,
½ glass of sherry,
2 lemons,
1 pint of hot water.

DIRECTIONS.—Cover gelatine with cold water; let soak one hour; add the hot water, and strain; add sugar, lemon juice, cranberry and sherry; set on ice till cold and serve with cream.

GRAPE JELLY—GOOD.

Take the grapes from the stem; put on in a kettle to cook, with only enough water to cover the bottom of the kettle; cook five minutes and strain through a thick jelly bag; have the sugar heating while the grapes are being prepared; put juice back on stove; boil and skim twenty minutes; add the sugar by degrees; cook one minute after it raises to a boil; pour in hot glasses and after they cool, put in a dark, cool place. Grapes used for jell should not be too ripe.

JELLY WITHOUT BOILING.

½ box of gelatine,
½ pint of cold water,
2 cups of white sugar,
2 lemons,
¼ teaspoon of cinnamon extract.

DIRECTIONS:—Add water to the gelatine; let stand an hour or more, then add the sugar and juice of the lemons and cinnamon and set on ice for a half day and it will be nice and firm; if any coloring is desired, use fruit coloring, but to serve with meats is nicer clear.

GREEN GRAPE JELLY

Choose grapes that are just beginning to ripen; cook with very little water; when cooked sufficient, put in a jelly bag and press lightly; let drain awhile and put in the kettle again and boil hard for twenty minutes; then add for every cup of juice one cup of white sugar, after heating, but be careful not to let it brown, as that will spoil the flavor as well as the looks of the jell; cook briskly for three minutes longer then put in hot jelly glasses and seal.

CURRANT JELLY.

Put the fruit on in a kettle; let heat slowly till the fruit is soft; then strain through a jelly bag and measure the juice and allow to one pint of juice ¾ of a pound of white sugar; put the juice on; boil hard and skim; when it has boiled fifteen minutes, add the sugar after heating it; cook five minutes longer and pour in glasses.

GREEN GOOSE BERRY JELLY.

Pick the stems from the berries; put to cook with a very little water; cook till soft; let cool and press through a jelly bag; add one pint of white sugar to every pint of juice; a small piece of alum dissolved and added makes it some nicer; put on stove and cook slowly till it will jell on a cool plate; be careful to skim well when it begins to boil and do not stir only enough to dissolve the sugar, as this spoils any kind of jelly; remove when done and pour in jelly glasses; have them dry and heated slightly; seal and keep in a dry place.

ORANGE JELLY.

½ box of gelatine,
½ cup of cold water,
1 cup of hot water,
2 cups of loaf sugar,
4 oranges,
1 lemon.

DIRECTIONS.—Soak the gelatine in the cold water; then pour over the hot water; squeeze the juice from the oranges and lemon; add the sugar and put in the gelatine; mix well and pour into wet molds, and set away to cool; when cold cut in squares and serve with whipped cream.

GRAPE BUTTER.

Choose very ripe grapes; pick from the stems; put to cook; when soft remove and cool, and press through a colander to remove the seeds; put in another kettle, about one-third of tart apples that you have grapes; cook till well done; press through a colander and mix the apples and grapes, and if desired, the skins of the grapes may be added, as they will cook up in the last heating; add three-quarters of a pound of sugar to one of pulp; cook slowly for three-quarters of an hour; put in jars and seal. They may have any kind of flavoring added that may be desired, but are quite nice without.

QUINCE MARMALADE.

Pare the quinces; slice thin, after coring them; put enough water over them to cook tender; mash and press through a sieve or colandar; put back on the stove, after weighing the fruit, and adding three-fourth of a pound of sugar to one of fruit; cook moderately fast for one-half an hour; put in jars and seal. Adding lemon or orange juice, adds some to the flavor, but if the quinces are nice, are very good with the flavor of the fruit only.

RHUBARB MARMALADE.

Take the rhubarb and cut in small pieces; put on in just enough water to cover the bottom of the kettle; cook till it will mash easily, then cool a little and press through a sieve; put back to cook, adding two cups of sugar to three cups of the pulp; cook till it begins to thicken, then put in glass jars and seal.

PUMPKIN BUTTER.

Take one large pumpkin, cook till well done, cool and press through a colander; put on to cook again, allowing one cup of sugar and one of molasses to every quart of the pumpkin; cook until it seems thoroughly done; flavor with ground cinnamon and spice. When made properly is very nice, and can be used for tarts, as well as served like any other kind of fruit butter.

PEACH JAM.

Allow three-fourths of a pound of sugar to a pound of peaches, after being peeled; cook till tender and will mash easily; add the sugar and cook for half an hour; after it begins to boil put in glass jars and seal.

CURRANT JAM.

Pick the currants over; free them from all leaves and stems; mash and press through a colander; then to every pound of fruit add three-fourths of a pound of white sugar; cook till it becomes very thick; put in jars and seal.

STRAWBERRY JAM

Choose nice clean berries; pick the stem from them; put in a colander and pour water over them to free them of sand and dirt; proceed to mash them and add the same amount of sugar to them as in currant jam; cook slowly for about ¾ of an hour, then put in jars and seal; put brandied paper over them; dip writing paper in brandy.

RASPBERRY AND CURRANT JAM.

Pick the raspberries and currants; clean them and mash together, then add the sugar, adding three-fouhts of a pound to a pound of fruit; cook for about three-quarters of an hour; remove and put in jars and seal; this makes a beautiful jam.

Raspberry jell may be made same as strawberry jell.

APPLE MARMALADE.

Take any kind of tart apples that cook easily; put on to cook in enough water to cover them; when cooked so they mash, remove and press through a colander and put back in the kettle and cook with three-quarters of a pound of sugar to one pound of apples; cook one and one-half hours and then put in jars, but is not necessary to seal, but always put writing paper over any jar that is not sealed, wet with brandy; do not put just a little, but saturate it thoroughly.

VINEGAR AND WINES.

RASPBERRY VINEGAR.

½ gallon of berries,
1 cup of vinegar,
1½ pints of sugar.

DIRECTIONS:—Pick and wash the berries; put them in an earthen jar; pour the vinegar over, then let stand three days; then strain and add the sugar and put in a kettle and boil twenty minutes, then bottle when cold; when going to use, use two tablespoons to a glass of water if used as a drink, and a tablespoon of sugar.

TO MAKE VINEGAR FROM CORN.

To one gallon of shelled corn, allow three gallons of water; soak the corn in just enough water to cover it, then boil in the other water till the corn begins to get tender; remove to a jar and put four gallons of boiling water over it and add one pint of molasses; let stand about two weeks and strain into a keg and soon it will be good vinegar.

TO MAKE APPLE VINEGAR.

Cut the apples up and put in a jar; do not remove the peel; cover with water, cold water is the best to use; then add to one gallon jar of apples, one pint of brown sugar and one quart of cold tea; molasses can be used instead of the sugar, but does not make as nice flavored or as clear vinegar; tie a cloth over the jar and let it remain a week; then skim it and strain into a keg, and put one pint of good vinegar to every gallon of the juice; do not fasten it up for two weeks, but put a thick cloth over the keg.

TO MAKE WINE FROM ANY KIND OF BERRIES.

For blackberry or raspberry wine, to each quart of the berries allow a pint of boiling water; let it remain over night; then strain, and to each quart of juice allow one pint of white sugar; let it remain in the jar ten days; then skim and strain into bottles and seal; it will be ready for use in six months. It is well to stir the juice several times a day, as this hastens the process of fermenting.

TO MAKE VINEGAR FROM HONEY.

To one pint of strained honey, put four quarts of hot water into a jar, and when it ferments, strain into jugs and it will make a very nice clear vinegar, and is preferred by some to any other vinegar.

CURRANT WINE.

This wine is made by stemming the currants, and allowing to every quart of the currants, three pints of water; mash before adding the water; let stand two days; then pass through a colander or sieve, and allow to every quart of juice one pound of sugar; dissolve thoroughly and put in a jug; let it remain ten or twelve days; then strain again and bottle for use. When putting in the jug do not put the cork in, but cover over with a cloth.

TO MAKE A GOOD WINE OF GRAPES.

To ten pounds of ripe grapes add three quarts of hot water; pick them from the stem, being careful not to have any that are not sound; put them in a stone jar, and after the water has cooled enough to handle with the hands, press them and remove the pulp and seeds; in this way let remain for four days; then strain and add five pounds of sugar, white sugar must be used; let it stand about six days; remove the scum; then strain again and bottle for use; it will be good in a month or so. Keep covered with a cloth while fermenting. This wine, when made properly, is fine.

PICKLES.

PEPPER MANGOES.

Use only the largest green peppers; make an incision in the side and remove the seed; put in salt water and let remain for twenty-four hours, have the water very strong with salt; chop nice white cabbage and season with white mustard seed, celery seed and salt, and put in a jar and cover with vinegar. Never use anything but the best of cider vinegar for pickles; put a small piece of alum in the vinegar in which the pickles are put, and cover over the top with green grape leaves, as this has a tendency to make them green; do not let the vinegar boil; they will be ready for use in a month or two.

SWEET GREEN CUCUMBER PICKLES.

Choose cucumbers about two inches long; put them in weak salt water; let stand twenty-four hours; then put on in a granite kettle; for one gallon pickles add one-half gallon sugar, one pint of the best apple vinegar, and one quart of water; let it boil ten minutes, after taking the pickles from the salt water; pour this boiling hot over the cucumbers; let stand twenty-four hours; heat again and pour over; then let stand the same time again, and when it is put on again, put in one tablespoon of cloves, one of spice and several sticks of cinnamon; let it boil; then pour on the cucumbers; put them in the jars and boil the syrup till thick; then pour over the pickles and let stand for three weeks before using. These are better if a half cup of whisky is added to they syrup when boiling the last time.

SWEET APPLE PICKLES.

Pare and core rather small apples; remove the core; if you have nothing to core fruit with, go to a tinner and get them to make one, by taking a small piece of tin, and make round, with an opening in the center, as large as desired, have it at least four inches long, as it will be needed some times for large fruit. After coring put in water till done paring and coring them; then make a syrup of three-fourths of a pound of sugar to one pound of the apples, allowing one quart of vinegar to one gallon of the syrup, one quart of the water to one-half pound of sugar; cook the syrup one-half an hour; then pour over the apples in a stone jar; repeat this three mornings; the fourth morning add the spices to the syrup and cook with the apples until they are tender; then skim them out into jars and boil the syrup for half an hour and pour over them and seal. Apples that do not cook up should be used for pickles.

GREEN TOMATO PICKLES.

Take medium sized tomatoes, be careful to have them entirely green, if they have begun to ripen it toughens them; slice and cover with salt and let stand two days; drain and put hot vinegar over them; let stand five days; then pour this off and heat fresh vinegar, and spices to taste; pour over the pickles and they will be ready for use in a week or two.

OLIVES.

Olives should be put on in a deep glass dish with cracked ice around them, as this makes them much nicer than without. Olives should remain on the table throughout the meal; they are often used to garnish with, same as pickles.

STRING BEAN PICKLES.

Choose well grown beans; but not those that have tough hulls; make a strong brine; let stand one week; take out and scald enough vinegar to cover them; add spices and pepper; they will be ready for use in two or three days after being put in the vinegar.

PICKLED CAULIFLOWER.

Pick off the leaves and cut the stalk in quarters; scald in salt water, but do not boil; take the cauliflower from the dish to cool; sprinkle with a little salt and water; put in a colander to drain; when well drained, then cut in small pieces and put on to boil in water salted slightly; when it comes to a boil skim out and put in jars; cover with vinegar which has been boiled with spices; seal up and it is ready for use in a few weeks.

TO PICKLE PEACHES.

3 pounds of sugar,
6 pounds of peaches,
1 tablespoon of cloves,
2 tablespoons of spice,
2 good sized sticks of cinnamon,
1 quart of vinegar.

DIRECTIONS:—Wash nice plum peaches; put in cold water and prepare the vinegar by putting in a porcelain kettle and adding sugar and spices; boil and skim; put peaches in a jar and pour vinegar over while hot; let stand twenty-four hours; then pour off and heat again and pour over; then repeat five times; then boil till quite a thick syrup; pour over and seal. If preferred the peaches may be peeled.

SPICED TOMATO PICKLES.

4 onions,
1 teaspoon of mace,
1 tablespoon of horse radish,
1 tablespoon of cloves,
2 quarts of tomatoes,
3 green peppers,
½ gallon of vinegar,
½ cup of salt.

DIRECTIONS.—Chop tomatoes and pepper fine; mix them together; put in a stone jar and sprinkle with the salt; let stand twenty-four hours; then drain through a colander; put the vinegar on to scald; add the spices and onions; when it comes to a boil pour over the pickles; pack in jars while hot and cover closely.

ONION PICKLES.

Take onions (white,) of uniform size and remove the outside peel; make a good brine; let it come to a boil, and pour over them; let remain in the brine two or three days; pour this off, and make a new brine; let them stand same length of time as before; take enough vinegar to cover the amount of onions you have, and two ounces of tumeric—this can be procured at any drug store; scald the vinegar, with this in it, and pour over the onions while very hot; let stand several days; then pour off and put hot vinegar, seasoned with celery seeds, white mustard seed, horse radish and mixed spices over them.

GREEN CUCUMBER CATSUP.

Take four good sized cucumbers; pare them deep; grate on a grater, but as they are a little difficult to grate, may be put in a chopping bowl and chopped sufficiently; after preparing them, put in a bag and squeeze slightly, and measure the cucumbers, and to every pint add one-fourth of a cup of grated horse radish, and some chopped onion may be added if preferred; season with salt and pepper; a few green peppers is an addition; after mixing well, add about one quart of good cider vinegar, mix and seal; it will be ready for use in a week or two.

RIPE TOMATO CATSUP.

One-half a peck of nice, ripe tomatoes; wash and slice them and add two good sized onions, chopped, and one large green pepper; cook all together till quite soft; then press through a sieve; wash the kettle and put them back to cook, and cook two hours, and add one cup of vinegar, one cup of sugar, one tablespoon of salt, two tablespoons of white mustard seed, one teaspoon of celery seed, one teaspoon each of cloves and spice, whole, two large sticks of cinnamon; tie these in a cloth, except the mustard and celery seed; cook one hour longer and bottle and seal.

SWEET PLUM PICKLES.

Use one peck of firm plums, not too ripe; scald them and skim out and have some jars ready; put in the jars; then heat one-half gallon vinegar, three pints of sugar, two tablespoons each of spice and cloves and two or three sticks of cinnamon; put the vinegar, spices and sugar on to cook, adding one quart of hot water; after boiling one hour pour over the plums and heat three mornings in succession; the last time put on, when it comes to a boil, put in the plums and let remain fifteen minutes; skim out into the cans and when the syrup is thick pour over and seal.

A NICE WAY TO PUT UP TOMATOES IN COLD VINEGAR.

Choose the plum tomatoes; select none but sound ones; put them in cans and pour over cold cider vinegar, but the vinegar must not be strong enough to eat the tomatoes; this can be ascertained by putting a little in a can and dropping some tomatoes into it a few days before canning and if is strong enough to eat the tomato, dilute with water; they must be sealed.

GRAPE CATSUP.

Put the grapes on to cook; cook till tender; then pass through a sieve and season with spices to suit the taste; cook twenty minutes, then add the vinegar; add about one quart to one-half gallon of the grape pulp and three cups of sugar; cook fifteen minutes longer and seal while hot. Nice to serve with boiled ham.

PLUM CATSUP.

Wash and put the plums on to cook in as little water as possible; when done, remove and when cool mash and press through a colander and add spice, cloves and cinnamon until it is flavored to suit taste, but a good porportion is, to one gallon of plums, add one tablespoon of cloves and two of each cinnamon and spice and one quart of good cider vinegar; mix well and bottle for use. This makes as large a quantity as would be needed for a small family. Is better after adding all of the ingredients to cook twenty minutes, as it will keep better.

SWEET PICKLED CHERRIES.

Choose ripe cherries, not too ripe, so they will stay on stem; lay on a platter; make a thick syrup of white sugar, then add one third as much vinegar as you have of the syrup; let come to the boiling point; have the cherries in a crock; pour this boiling hot over them; next morning pour off and heat again; repeat four mornings, the fourth morning let it come to a boil, then add the cherries; let them cook five minutes; remove to the jar and boil the syrup till done, till it is moderately thick, putting cloves, cinnamon and spice, the whole tied up in a cloth till the strength is extracted enough, then pour over the cherries and seal.

Toilet Recipes.

A GOOD REMEDY FOR FRECKLES.

Two ounces of alum, three ounces of lemon juice, one pint of rose water; apply with a sponge at night.

TO REMOVE MOTH PATCHES.

Fifteen grains of chlorate of potash; put in four ounces of rose water and let it remain a few days. Is excellent to remove moth patches from the face; apply several times during the day with a sponge or old linen rag.

A GOOD WASH FOR THE HAIR.

One quart of tea made from the hulls of the common walnut; they should be used while partially green. After straining into a bottle; add to this three ounces of copperas; let stand several days before using, then apply with a brush; shake the bottle before using; this will never fail to color the hair and is perfectly harmless and can be prepared at home.

A GOOD LIQUID TO CLEAN SILVER.

Take equal parts of prepared chalk, aqua ammonia and alcohol; mix these well together; put in a bottle; when using, apply with a sponge and polish with a chamois skin. This will clean silver thoroughly and if properly used, a fine polish can be made equal to new silver.

A TONIC FOR THE HAIR.

Is made by steeping a handful of sage in one quart of soft water; after steeping for half an hour, add one tablespoon of common table salt; strain into a bottle and apply to the hair, once a week, rubbing in the scalp well. It not only causes the hair to grow, but darkens it with a few applications, also prevents it from falling out.

HOW TO CLEAN GOLD.

Use pulverized chalk, castile soap and warm soft water; shave the soap and add the chalk, dissolved thoroughly; then with a soft brush proceed to wash the gold articles; rub well and they will look like new.

TO REMOVE SPOTS, PIMPLES, ETC.

A piece of green benzoin about the size of a pea, one small glass of spirits of wine; boil these together for half an hour. To use, put ten drops in a glass of soft water; wash the face and hands in this twice a day. When poured in water it looks like milk and has a sweet perfume.

FOR THE COMPLEXION.

½ pint of oatmeal,
1 pint of buttermilk,
1 lemon.

DIRECTIONS.—Steep the oatmeal and milk together and let it cool before adding the lemon juice; apply at night before retiring. This will be found excellent for removing tan and softening the skin.

A SURE REMEDY TO REMOVE WARTS.

Use pure carbolic acid; apply with a brush three times a day, being careful not to touch any other part of the hand, as it would be like a burn. This will cure a wart in a few days.

A REMEDY TO PREVENT REDNESS OF THE NOSE AND FACE.

Equal parts of refined chalk, rain-water and glycerine, made into a paste—apply and remove in the morning with a soft cloth and warm water.

TO REMOVE DANDRUFF.

Take equal parts of Bay Rum and Brandy and brush the hair every day—wash the head thoroughly once a week with soft water and yolk of an egg; this followed for at least one month will effectually cure dandruff, and is certainly a very simple remedy and one that is in reach of all.

TO CLEAN THE TEETH.

The following will be found excellent. A small piece of orris root chewed after rinsing the mouth after meals cleanses the teeth perfectly, removes any discoloration from eating fruits. Burned bread is good to clean the teeth; burn it till it is well charred. The use of a poor brush ruins the gums and makes them look ragged.

ANOTHER REMEDY TO WHITEN THE COMPLEXION

Is a paste made as follows: Take two tablespoons of common tar and one tablespoon of olive oil; melt this together until well mixed; spread on an old linen cloth and apply to the face on retiring; care has to be taken to prevent the bed clothing from getting soiled; in the morning remove the cloth and wash the face with castile soap; the face will be soft and white.

TO PREVENT SUNSTROKE.

A wet handkerchief or brown paper well saturated with water worn in the top of the hat will prevent sunstroke, no matter how much one is exposed to the sun, as it has no effect if protected in this way.

TO MAKE A GOOD COLOGNE WATER.

One-half a pint of alcohol, thirty drops of bergamont, thirty drops of essence of lemon, thirty drops of orange water; mix together and bottl. Will be ready for use in six weeks.

TO MAKE GOOD QUALITY OF COLOGNE.

One pint of rectified spirit, one fluid drachm each of oil of bergamont and lemon; one-half drachm of oil of orange; one quarter of a drachm of neroli; two drops of the essence of ambergris and musk; mix all well together and bottle and let it ripen for several months before using; is better not to use it under three months. This, if made right is excellent.

TO MAKE A GOOD COLD CREAM.

3 ounces of oil of almonds,
1 ounce of spermaceti,
1 drachm of the best white wax,
3 ounces of rose water,
½ ounce of white rose perfume.

DIRECTIONS:—Melt the wax and mix with the oil; add the rose water and perfume; stir till it is cold and creamy and it is ready for use. Is nice to use on the face or hands to soften the skin. Is also good to remove tan.

TO MAKE LAVENDER POWDER.

One half a pound of powdered lavender, one-eighth of a pound of gum of benzonia, the same of otto of lavender; mix well together and it is ready for use.

TO MAKE HELIOTROPE POWDER.

One-fourth of a pound of orris root, one-eighth of a pound of powdered rose leaves, one ounce of powdered tonquin bean, one-half an ounce of vanilla bean, one-half a drachm of musk in the grain, two drops of otto of almonds. Mix thoroughly together and this is one of the best satchet powders made and the cost will not be much. Is nice to put in the linens.

FOR PRESPIRATION OF THE HANDS.

A remedy for anyone who is bothered with their hands prespiring: The white of one egg, beaten stiff; then add one ounce of powdered alum and one cup of wheat bran; mix well. After washing the hands and drying them, apply some of the paste; let it remain for awhile and rub off with a soft cloth. This will soften the hands and check the prespiration, which sometimes is very annoying.

TO CURE A MUDDY COMPLEXION

Extract the juice from one lemon; put in a glass of soft water ten drops of attar of roses; use every time the face is washed; put on freely and let remain. This will be found an excellent remedy for a muddy complexion, of which, unfortunately, so many American ladies are possessed.

Miscellaneous for the House.

TO KEEP APPLES.

Apples may be kept till the last of June by being careful to select the sound ones; wipe them perfectly dry and pack them in boxes or barrels, whichever is the most convenient, with layers of bran, then of apples, then cover the barrel or box over with a cloth to keep the moisture absorbed, as the cloth absorbs the moisture, and that is what causes the fruit to decay.

WOODEN PAILS

May be rendered more servicable by giving them a good coat of varnish before using and letting it dry several days before putting water in it. A bucket treated in this way lasts much longer than without.

TO REMOVE INK STAINS.

They can be removed with sweet milk from carpets, after rinsing with clean soft water. If on goods dip in melted tallow and wash the goods with very hot water, dipping in and out of the water, as it ought to be so hot that the grease may be removed with the stain. Salt is also said to remove ink stains. Put on immediately the ink is spilled, but on any delicate frabric, care must be taken or the ink will spread rapidly.

TO SWEETEN LARD.

To sweeten lard after it has become strong, tie a small bunch of slippery elm bark; melt the lard and add the bark; boil an hour or more; then remove the bark, and your lard will seem almost as fresh as when first rendered.

TO OIL A FLOOR.

Used boiled linseed oil; before using, heat it again, and after heating, and it has been removed from the stove, if a light oak color is desired, put in some yellow ochre; mix it well. It will cause the oil to boil over if put in while on the stove, and would be very dangerous. If a dark floor is desired, use burnt umber, as this makes a very pretty stain. It will be necessary, if the floor is rough, to give it a second coating, otherwise one application will be sufficient.

HOW TO CLEAN MICA.

This often becomes very smoky from use, and presents an ugly appearance, but it can be cleaned very easily, by washing in strong vinegar, and in most stoves is easily removed and in this way is more conveniently cleaned.

HOW TO CLEAN A SPONGE.

Take a lemon; roll it till soft; then cut off a small piece from one end; squeeze the juice into the sponge; wash it in this till the sponge is well saturated; then rinse in several waters. The juice is so acid that it cuts the dirt better than soap. It will cleanse it thoroughly.

ALUM WATER FOR COCK ROACHES.

Cock roaches will not inhabit any place where alum water has been used, as alum is very offensive to them. Dissolve some alum in water and wash the wood work around the kitchen and shelves in the pantry and safe once a week and no roaches will make their appearance.

TO WASH CHINA.

In washing china, never pour boiling water over it, as it will make it soon crack and have an old appearance, and can be cleaned as well in moderately warm water and dried thoroughly.

COAL ASHES

Make good walks for the back yard or can be used in the garden, as one advantage is, no weeds will grow up through them.

TO MAKE CARPETS BRIGHT.

Keep tea leaves for this purpose; sprinkle the carpet before sweeping, sweep off lightly at first, then go over the floor with a dry cloth to remove all dust; if there are grease spots on carpet, put a thick brown paper over it and set a very warm iron on it and let remain several minutes. Remove, and the paper will have absorbed all, or the most of the grease.

TO CLEAN LAMPS.

First, lamps should have the oil emptied from them frequently and thoroughly cleaned, as by letting lamps collect too much dust, sometimes causes an explosion. Also clean the burners, by putting them in strong soda water. An old tin can can be utilized to soak them in. Soapsuds will answer instead of soda. They will come out quite new and make an entirely different light. It well pays for the trouble.

TO CLEAN SILVER.

Saturate a woolen cloth with coal oil and dip into whitening; then rub your silver and it will look like new. No matter how long it has been used, provided it is not worn off any.

TO KEEP AN OILED FLOOR LOOKING NEW.

To keep an oiled floor looking like new, wipe it up with water, not too hot, diluted with sour milk, as this keeps the lustre on the floor a long time, if it is too much trouble to use beeswax, which is better than anything else.

TO REMOVE MACHINE GREASE.

To remove machine grease from goods, either fresh lard, well rubbed in, or soda dissolved in soft water, will remove machine grease.

TO REMOVE FLY SPECKS

To remove fly specks from any article of furniture, wet with a soft brush dipped in any good wine and apply. Will always remove them without injuring the furniture.

TO REMOVE GREASE FROM MARBLE.

Take powdered chalk and put a thick coat over the grease spot; take a hot lid from the stove and hold over it for a few minutes, when you can see that the chalk has absorbed the grease, and it can be easily brushed off.

TO REMOVE SOOT FROM CARPETS.

Sprinkle with salt before sweeping, and when the carpet is swept no trace of the soot can be be found.

TO PREVENT STEEL FROM RUSTING.

By dusting steel with unslacked lime, after it has been cleaned, will prevent it from rusting and is very easily applied.

TO KEEP CELLARS FROM SMELLING MUSTY.

Take copperas and dissolve it in hot water, and go over the walls, as you would in giving it a coat of white wash. This is a good disinfectant, as well as good to keep away rats and mice.

COLD STARCH.

It is greatly improved by mixing the starch with soap suds. Do not have the suds too strong, and rub your irons with sandpaper, before commencing to iron, and there will be no starch sticking to the irons and a nice gloss will be the result if the directions are followed in mixing the starch and preparing the iron. Always use hot water in mixing cold starch, but do not have it scalding.

TO PERFUME NOTE PAPER.

Take an ordinary sized blotter; saturate it with any kind of good perfume; put in the box with the note paper and keep the box closed and you will be surprised at how nicely your paper is perfumed, and it will retain a perfume for a long time.

TO POLISH STOVES.

In polishing stoves, soap suds mixed with stove polish makes a a better lustre and they are more easily polished.

TO RENEW OLD CHANDELIERS.

Apply copal varnish, in which some bronze powder has been added; mix well and apply with a brush and it will help it wonderfully.

A POLISH FOR BRASS OR COPPER KETTLES.

To polish a brass or copper kettle take lemon and salt; cut the lemon in two pieces; dip in the salt and rub the kettle well. It will make them very bright, and is easily applied.

TO REMOVE BLOOD STAINS.

Dip in kerosene and let remain awhile; then wash the stains out with cold water. It will never fail to remove them.

TO MAKE BLACK CASSIMERE LOOK LIKE NEW.

Take one-fourth cup of ammonia to one quart of soft water; sponge the pieces well with a clean sponge; roll up tight in a clean cloth and iron immediately on a flannel cloth; be sure to iron on the wrong side of the cloth; have the iron rather hot and iron until perfectly dry; afterwards brush well if any lint adheres to the cloth and you will think yourself doubly repaid for your work, as the goods can scarcely be told from new goods.

A GOOD DISINFECTANT FOR CELLARS.

Use chloride of lime in old dishes; set around in the cellar; also sprinkle the floor with a strong solution of copperas once a month and your cellar will be kept free from any bad odor.

TO DRIVE MOSQUITOES

From the room, burn powered pyrethum on a shovel or put some coals in a pan and sprinkle the powder over it and the insects will vacate the place in a very short time.

TO FILTER WATER.

Take a large earthen jar; soak in water several days; then put a sponge in the hole at the bottom, which must be made as large as the bottom of a teacup; fill this with sand about half way up, and the other half fill in with coarse gravel; let the water pass through this and it will be well filtered. The sponge must be removed every few days and cleaned, but the sand and gravel will last several days without being renewed.

TO KEEP A ROOM MOIST.

A large sponge thoroughly saturated with cold water and suspended by a string and hung in a room, will aid materially in keeping the air in the room cool and moist. Can be hung behind something if desired, and will serve the same purpose.

TO KEEP AWAY FLIES.

Leaves from a walnut tree kept in the kitchen will keep away flies. It is necessary to renew them every two or three days.

TO SET COLOR.

To set a color when coloring, use oxgall, dissolved in soft water, using two tablespoons to every pint of water. Sweet milk is also good to set the color in black goods, or in any dark color, by immersing the goods in the milk when removed from the dye, and covering it closely for at least two hours, then rinsing in several waters to remove all the milk. Goods treated in this way will never rub off in making or wearing.

TO REMOVE GREASE FROM A FLOOR.

To remove grease from a floor, make a paste of clay and put on the grease spot; leave on over night; then wash off with hot water; after first brushing the clay off; use white sand to wash with, in the place of soap, and in most cases you will not see any grease, but if it is not removed entirely, make another application.

TO BLEACH MUSLIN.

Take one tablespoon of oxalic acid to one gallon of water; put the muslin in a tub and pour this over it; let remain until the water is cold; then put out on the grass. This will soon bleach the muslin till it will be as white as bleached muslin. The acid is cheap and can be procured from any druggist.

TO CLEAN WHITE ZEPHYR.

Take equal parts of flour and magnesia; rub as if washing in water. If the article is very much soiled it may be necessary to change for fresh flour and magnesia, but if properly used, will cleanse the article perfectly, and it will look as nice as when new.

TO REMOVE MILDEW.

Mix soap and chalk together; rub in well; keep in the hot sun; keep moist and the mildew will disappear.

TO PREVENT MOTH IN CARPETS.

Take a piece of paper and cover it with pitch; let it dry and place under the edges of the carpet and it will render the carpet moth proof. The odor may be unpleasant for awhile but not more so than having the carpets eaten up by moth.

TO KEEP MILK PAILS AND PANS FRESH AND SWEET.

After washing them, rinse well with charcoal powder dissolved in water. Kept in a glass jar is more convenient and always ready for use.

TO TIGHTEN CANE SEATED CHAIRS.

Turn the chair over and wash thoroughly with warm soap suds and it will, when dry, be as tight and firm as when new if the cane has not been broken.

TO REMOVE OLD PAINT.

Give it a washing with a swab of a solution of oxalic acid. Weak tea is good to wash paint that has been varnished as it will look like new if properly washed.

A DRESSING FOR KID SHOES.

Oil and ink mixed together makes a good dressing for kid shoes. Makes them black and keeps them soft.

A GOOD CEMENT FOR GLASS.

Is made by taking equal parts of sweet milk and vinegar, boiling them together and separating the curd that will form, or strain it, and beat the whites of several eggs, say to one pint of whey, the whites of four eggs, beaten stiff; mix together and add enough lime, powdered well, to make a paste. Is excellent for mending broken glass; this can be put in hot water and it does not affect it in the least.

CEMENT FOR JARS OR BOTTLES.

Use one tablespoon of beeswax to three tablespoons of resin; melt together till well mixed. Glass jars that have a piece broken out of them can be mended easily in this way.

WASHING FLUID.

1 pound of sal soda,
½ pound of lime,
6 quarts of water.

DIRECTIONS:—Put this together on the stove in an iron kettle; boil ten minutes, then remove and strain into jars. One-half a cup of this added to a boiler of water will soften it nicely, and the clothes will wash much more easily.

TO REMOVE IRON RUST

From white goods, equal parts of salt and lemon juice is good; expose to the sun awhile, or till it is dry. Sometimes it requires several applications.

TO REMOVE SCORCH FROM LINEN.

Exposeure to the sun while it is very hot will nearly always remove it, unless scorched too deep.

TO RENOVATE BLACK SILK.

Sponge with coffee and iron with a hot iron before it is quite dry, being careful to iron on wrong side, but sponge it on the right side.

TO CLEAN KETTLES.

Potato peelings put in new kettles and boiled for some time with plenty of water, will clean them perfectly clean. They are also good to clean porcelain, if it has turned brown from use.

TO KEEP CIDER SWEET.

To keep cider sweet for quite awhile: A piece of charcoal dropped in the barrel, or some white mustard seed. It will take a pint and a half to a barrel of cider.

WHEN MAKING SOAP

It is much nicer to remove from the iron kettle, as it is more clear than to cool in the iron, especially if it is to be cut in bars. Oil of sassafras put in soap when it is almost ready to remove from the fire, gives it a very nice perfume.

TO POLISH TINWARE.

Use soda dampened slightly for polishing tinware, as it will if properly used and rubbed with either a woolen cloth or a chamois skin be almost like new.

A GOOD FURNITURE POLISH.

One that every one can prepare at home: Take one pint of good turpentine and two pints of linseed oil; mix well together and apply with an old woolen cloth and the furniture will not only have a new appearance, but it will restore the color if it has turned white in spots where anything hot has been set on it, or from getting damp.

TO CLEAN SOAP SUDS

This can be done by taking some alum and dissolving it in hot water and putting in the suds; it will curdle and all the dirt will settle at the bottom and the water can be poured off and it will be as clear as before using and will do double the amount washing. This is very valuable to any one who is scarce of good washing water.

CISTERNS

In which the water has an unpleasant odor or taste may be purified by throwing a pound of charcoal into it; in a few days the disagreeable odor will leave. Charcoal is good to keep in refrigerators also.

MENUS.

MENU FOR BREAKFAST, NO. 1.

1st Course—Oranges and Grapes.
2nd Course—Broiled Fish, Saratoga Potatoes.
Coffee and Tea.
3rd Course—Mutton Chops, with Tomato Sauce.
4th Course—Omelet, garnished with Parsley.
5th Course—Cream Toast and Muffins.
6th Course—Graham Pancakes and Syrup.

MENU FOR BREAKFAST, NO. 2

Oranges.   Tea.   Coffee.
Cream Potatoes.   Mutton Chops.
Cheese Toast.   Rice Pancakes.
Maple Syrup.

MENU FOR BREAKFAST, NO. 3.

Beef Steak.   Fried Potatoes.
Light Rolls.   Cream Toast.
Coffee.

MENU FOR BREAKFAST, NO. 4.

Corn Meal Cakes.
Stewed Mackerel, with Fish Sauce.
Baked Potatoes.   Poached Eggs.
Maple Syrup.
Chocolate.   Coffee.

MENU FOR AFTERNOON RECEPTIONS.

Boiled Tongue.
Pressed Chicken.   Oyster Salad.
Potato Croquettes.   Chocolate Cream.
Whipped Cream.
Fancy Cakes.
Fruit.   Coffee.   Cocoa.
Lemonade.

Menu for Thanksgiving Dinner.

∽o∽

Roast Turkey, with Oyster Sauce.

Cranberry Sauce.

Mashed Turnips.

Squash.

Boiled Onions.   Potatoes.

Dressed Celery.

Chicken Pie, with Jelly.

Mince Pie.   Apple Pie.

Cranberry Tarts.

Lemon Squash Pie.

Nuts.   Fruits.   Raisins.

Candy.   Coffee.

Cider.

Menu for Thanksgiving Dinner, No. 2.

Raw Oysters.   Clear Soup.

Roast Turkey, with Cranberry Sauce.

Mashed Potatoes.

Sweet Potatoes.   Parsnips.   Turnips.

Pickles.   Celery.

Peas.   Croquettes.

Lettuce, with Mayonnaise.

Mince Pie.   Pumpkin Pie.

Coffee.   Cocoa.

Fruit Cake.

MENU FOR DINNER, NO. 1.

Soup.

Oyster Stew.   Olives.   Sliced Lemons.
Celery Branches.   Pickles.

Fish.

Baked White Fish, with Chili Sauce.
Boiled Ham, with Horse Radish Sauce.

Roasts.

Beef Roast, with Potato Chips.
Baked Turkey, with Cranberry Sauce.
Roast Duck.   Apple Sauce.
Pigs' feet with Green Peas.

Entrees.

Corn Muffins.   Chicken Salad.
Oyster Patties.   Gibblets in cream.
Boston Baked Beans.

Vegetables.

Lima Beans.   Green Beans.
Sweet Corn.   Fried Cabbage.
Baked Sweet Potatoes.   Mashed Irish Potatoes.

Relishes.

Grape Jelly.   Sweet Peach Pickles.
Saratoga Chips.   French Capers.
Salted Almonds.   Mixed Pickles.

Dessert.

Mince Pie.   Lemon Pie.   Chess Pie.
Steamed Plum Pudding, with Brandy Sauce.
Ice Cream Cake.   Angle Cake.
Chocolate Cake.   Fruit Cake.
Vanilla Ice Cream.
Oranges.   Grapes.   Bananas.
Coffee.   Tea.   Milk.   Ice Tea.

MENU FOR DINNER, NO. 2.

Potato Soup.
Bread.
Boiled Fish,   Oyster Soup.
Escalloped Potatoes.
Roast Chicken.   Brown Gravy.
Baked Sweet Potatoes.
Green Beans.
Lettuce.   Salad.   Olives.   Cheese.
Ice Cream.
Cake.   Coffee.

MENU FOR DINNER, NO. 3.

Sliced Tomatoes.
Roast Beef.   Celery.
Mashed Irish Potatoes,   Baked Sweet Potatoes.
Cabbage, fried.   Olives.
Chicken Salad.
Graham Bread.
Bread Pudding, with Sauce.
Whipped Cream, with small Cakes.
Coffee and Cocoa.

MENU FOR DINNER, NO. 4.

Clear Soup.   Celery.
Baked Fish.   Lettuce Salad.
Roast Mutton.   Fried Chicken.

Vegetables.
Asparagus.   Peas.   Potatoes.   Squash.

Dessert.
Plum Pudding.   Sliced Apple Pie.
Strawberries and Cream.
Coffee and Cheese.

MENU FOR A CHRISTMAS DINNER.

Soup.   Celery.
Roast Turkey.
Potato Croquettes.   Baked Sweet Potatoes.
Cranberry Sauce.
Birds on Toast.
Corn.   Peas.   Pickles.   Plum Jelly.
Plum Pudding.
Mince Pie.   Cream Pie.
Cheese.   Fruits.   Nuts.
Coffee.   Fruit Cake.

MENU FOR LUNCHEON, NO. 1.

Orange Sherbet.
Baked Chicken.   White House Rolls.
Salted Almonds.   Olives.
Boiled Beef.   Green Peas.   Biscuit.
Lobster Salad.   Wafers.   Cheese.
Strawberry Short Cake, with Whipped Cream.
Coffee.
Grapes on stem.   Angel Food.
Ice Cream.
Cocoa.   Tea.

MENU FOR LUNCHEON, NO. 2.

Chicken Croquettes.
Potatoes, Baked.
Boiled Ham, Oyster Salad.   Rolls.
Fruit.   Small Cakes.
Tea and Cocoa.

MENU FOR LUNCHEON, NO. 3.

Raw Oysters.
Bouillon, served in cups.
Lamb Chops.   Tomato Sauce.
Chicken Croquettes.   Green Peas.
Quail on Toast.
Potato Salad.
Wafers.   Cheese.
Ice Cream.
Cake.   Fruit.   Coffee.

Remarks On Garnishing.

Any kind of salads are nice garnished with either of the following:

EGG RINGS.

These are made by cutting the whites of hard boiled eggs round ways; put around the salad and on top.

LEMONS.

Slice the lemons very thin after removing the outside rind and seeds; place around cold meats, either pork, beef, canned salmon or chicken.

CELERY HEARTS AND LEAVES.

These are used to garnish with, and are very nice for all kinds of meat.

OLIVES AND PICKLES.

Sliced thin these are also used for salads and meats. Any kind of tart jelly can be molded in very small glasses and put over and around the meat. Sprigs of parsley are also used.

BOILED BEETS.

Potato salad looks very pretty garnished with thin slices of boiled beets.

BAKING APPLES FOR PORK ROAST.

Pare some good baking apples, and put in a baking pan; put some butter and sugar over them, and enough water to make a sauce around them; when well done remove the apples and put around the roast; add some brandy to the sauce and serve with the roast.

POTATO BALLS.

Roast turkey garnished with potato balls made of creamed mashed potatoes. Make into small balls and put in a baking pan, brush over with some sweet cream, and put in a brisk oven till a nice brown; remove and put around the turkey, and serve with cream gravy.

FOR PUDDINGS.

Puddings garnished with fruit, candied cherries, oranges or lemons impart a nice flavor, as well as improve the looks of any kind of puddings; after the pudding is put in the dishes, garnish with the candied fruit and send to the table.

Ice cream that is molded is very nice garnished with strawberries, or any kind of small fruit.

Allowance for Entertainments.

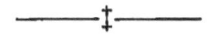

A few suggestions on making an allowance for entertainments, either public or in the home:

    1 gallon of fresh oysters,
    1 turkey, weighing 10 pounds,
    1 small ham,
    2 chickens, for salad,
    1½ dozen sandwiches,
    1 quart of cranberry sauce,
    ½ gallon of pickles,
    ½ gallon of ice cream.

This allowance is for twelve persons, and can be increased or diminished according to the number of persons to be served. Will serve as a help to those that are not accustomed to this kind of work.

TABLE OF MEASURES AND WEIGHTS.

1 heaping quart of flour weighs............1 pound.
4 teacups of flour weighs.................1 pound.
1 quart of meal after sifting weighs.........1 pound 4 oz.
1 pint soft butter weighs..................1 pound.
2 teacups of soft butter weighs.............1 pound.
1½ pints of sugar weighs..................1 pound.
2 coffee cups of sugar weighs..............1 pound.
7 tablespoons of sugar equals.............1 cup.
5 tablespoons of flour equals.............1 cup.
4 tablespoons of soft butter equals.........1 cup.
3 tablespoons of grated chocolate weighs ..1 oz.
2 heaping teaspoons of sugar or flour.........1 tablespoon.

LIQUIDS.

1 pint contains............16 fluid ounces or 4 gills.
1 ounce equals...........8 fluid drachms or ¼ gill.
1 tablespoon contains..............½ fluid ounce.
1 teaspoon equal..................1 fluid drachm.
4 teaspoons equals..................1 tablespoon.
16 tablespoons equal..................½ of a pint.
1 wine glass equals..................4 tablespoons.
1 teacup equals..........................2 gills.
4 teacups equal..........................1 quart.
1 common sized tumbler holds..............½ pint.

DEPARTMENTS.

	PAGE.
Bread	5
Meats	23
Poultry and Game	37
Fish and Oysters	45
Soups	52
Sauces and Gravies	59
Salads	67
Eggs and Omelets	75
Sandwiches	84
Vegetables	87
Puddings and Dumplings	109
Pies	122
Layer Cakes	145
Loaf Cakes	160
Cookies	187
Fancy Dishes	196
Miscellaneous for the Table	211
Hot and Cold Drinks	203
Creams and Ices	217
Candy Making at Home	225
Canned and Dried Fruits	231
Miscellaneous Recipes	239

Preserves, Jells and Jams..................250
Vinegar and Wines 262
Pickles 265
Toilet Recipes...........................273
Miscellaneous for the House..............279
Menus....................................292
Remarks on Garnishing....................297
Allowance for Entertainments.............299
Table of Measures and Weights............300

www.ingramcontent.com/pod-product-compliance
Lightning Source LLC
Chambersburg PA
CBHW030818230426
43667CB00008B/1270